LUDWIG VON MISES

LIBRARY OF MODERN THINKERS

SERIES EDITOR: JEFFREY O. NELSON

PUBLISHED TITLES

ROBERT NISBET *by Brad Lowell Stone*

LUDWIG VON MISES *by Israel M. Kirzner*

FORTHCOMING

WILHELM RÖPKE *by John Zmirak*

ERIC VOEGELIN *by Michael P. Federici*

MICHAEL OAKESHOTT *by Timothy Fuller*

BERTRAND DE JOUVENAL *by Daniel Mahoney*

ANDREW LYTLE *by Mark Malvasi*

FRANCIS GRAHAM WILSON *by H. Lee Cheek*

WILL HERBERG *by Vigen Guroian*

LUDWIG
VON MISES

THE MAN AND HIS ECONOMICS

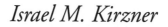

Israel M. Kirzner

NEW YORK UNIVERSITY

ISI Books

Wilmington, Delaware

2001

The Library of Modern Thinkers is published in cooperation with Collegiate Network, Inc. Generous grants from the Sarah Scaife Foundation, Earhart Foundation, F. M. Kirby Foundation, Castle Rock Foundation, Pierre F. and Enid Goodrich Foundation, Wilbur Foundation, and the William H. Donner Foundation made this series possible. The Intercollegiate Studies Institute and Collegiate Network, Inc., gratefully acknowledge their support.

Cataloging-in-Publication Data

Kirzner, Israel M.
    Ludwig von Mises: the man and his economics /
    by Israel M. Kirzner.—
    1st ed.—Wilmington, Del. : ISI Books, 2001.

    p. cm. (Library of modern thinkers)

    ISBN 1-882926-61-7 (cloth) —ISBN 1-882926-68-4 (PBK).
    1. Von Mises, Ludwig, 1881-1973 . 2. Economists—Austria—biography. 3. Austrian school of Economics. I. Title. II. Series.

HB101.v66 K57 2001   01-110950
330.157/092 B—dc21   CIP

Published in the United States by:

    ISI Books
    In cooperation with Collegiate Network, Inc.
    Post Office Box 4431
    Wilmington, DE 19807-0431

Cover and interior design by Sam Torode
Manufactured in the United States of America

B'EZRAS HASHEM

CONTENTS

ABBREVIATIONS AND REFERENCES

ALL PAGE REFERENCES in the text are to the writings of Mises and his wife. When referring to his books, I use the following abbreviations. All other references are in the endnotes.

EFI   *Economic Freedom and Interventionism: An Anthology of Articles and Essays by Ludwig von Mises,* ed. Bettina Bien-Greaves (Irvington-on-Hudson: Foundation for Economic Education, 1990).

EP   *Economic Policy: Thoughts for Today and Tomorrow* (South Bend, Ind.: Regnery Gateway, 1979).

EPE   *Epistemological Problems of Economics* (Princeton, N.J.: Van Nostrand, 1960).

HA   *Human Action: A Treatise on Economics,* 3rd revised edition (Chicago: Henry Regnery, 1966).

HSAS   *The Historical Setting of the Austrian School of Economics* (New Rochelle, N.Y.: Arlington House, 1969).

LCT   *Liberalism in the Classical Tradition* (San Francisco: Foundation for Economic Education and Cobden Press, 1985).

NR   *Notes and Recollections,* trans. Hans F. Sennholz (South Holland, Ill.: Libertarian Press, 1978).

MMC   *On the Manipulation of Money and Credit,* ed. Percy L. Greaves and trans. Bettina Bien-Greaves (Dobbs Ferry, N.Y.: Free Market Books, 1978).

MMMP   *Money, Method, and the Market Process: Essays by Ludwig von Mises,* ed. Richard M. Ebeling (Norwell, Mass.: Praxeology Press of the Ludwig von Mises Institute, and Kluwer Academic Publications, 1990).

MYWM   *My Years with Ludwig von Mises* (New Rochelle, N.Y.: Arlington House, 1976).

S   *Socialism: An Economic and Sociological Analysis,* trans. J. Kahane (London: Jonathan Cape, 1936).

TH   *Theory and History: An Interpretation of Social and Economic Revolution* (New Haven: Yale University Press, 1957).

TMC   *The Theory of Money and Credit,* rev. edition (New Haven: Yale University Press, 1953).

UFES   *The Ultimate Foundation of Economic Science: An Essay on Method* (Princeton, N.J.: Van Nostrand, 1962).

PREFACE

THIS WORK is certainly not a full-length biography (nor even an intellectual biography) of Ludwig von Mises. What I have sought to present, in briefest outline, is the *story of Mises in his role of economist*. In attempting to provide this outline, I have faced certain difficulties which, not at all coincidentally, arose out of the very deep personal significance to me of telling this story. Ludwig von Mises was my revered teacher. Everything I have learned, taught, or written, in and on economics, derives, to greater or lesser extent, from what I learned close to a half-century ago in his classes and seminars at New York University, and from what I have learned during these past forty-six years from his published writings. Mises suffered severe professional rejection during the closing decades of his career. As my own understanding of economics has deepened over time, my awareness of this professional rejection has also deepened, in turn, the respect and affection with which I regard my teacher. And it is, of course, precisely this regard and affection which render it a virtual impossibility to hope that my story of Mises, the economist, can be a strictly impartial and objective one. Yet surely Mises, that stern exemplar of intellectual honesty, would have insisted that his story be told with complete candor and detachment. The standards of intellectual integrity which Mises represented are simply inconsistent with any hagiographic treatment.

I have done my best to present Mises and his economics without, on the one hand, concealing my own admiration for the subtlety and depth of Misesian economics, and, on the other hand, without failing to take note of the difficulties which other economists (and sometimes even Mises' own followers) have encountered in that work.

A number of scholars have explored various aspects of Mises' intellectual contributions and legacy. All students of Misesian economics must be grateful to Bettina Bien-Greaves for her remarkable two-volume *Mises: An Annotated Bibliography,* a veritable treasure house of information. Professor Richard Ebeling has devoted most of his scholarly career to the study of the life and work of Mises. He has contributed a number of superb introductions to several volumes of Mises' writings, which he also discovered and edited. Professor Ebeling's forthcoming full-length biography of Mises is eagerly awaited. Eamonn Butler has attempted an ambitious survey of Mises' overall intellectual contribution (from a somewhat different point of departure than that taken in the present work). Professor Karen Vaughn, in the course of her notable exploration of a broader, fascinating episode in intellectual history (*Austrian Economics in America: The Migration of a Tradition* [Cambridge: Cambridge University Press, 1994]), has dealt significantly (and critically) with important segments of Mises' career. The late Murray N. Rothbard, brilliant American disciple of Mises, has more than once presented his own appreciation of Mises' work. And Rothbard's own extraordinarily prolific published writings constitute—even where one feels compelled to disagree with aspects of those writings—a remarkable testimony to Mises' influence and inspiration. Others, too, (including, especially, scholars working with the Auburn University–based Ludwig von Mises Institute) have made significant additions to Mises scholarship. And I have no doubt that the years ahead will bring many more contributions to this fascinating area of intellectual history. It gives me great personal satisfaction to be able to add my own modest contribution to this literature.

I wish to thank Mr. Jeffrey O. Nelson, publisher of ISI Books, for suggesting this project to me and for encouraging me to pursue it. I am particularly grateful to my colleagues in the Austrian Economics Program at New York University, Professor Mario J. Rizzo and Dr. David Harper, for their contributions to this volume. Each of them gave me advice and encouragement during the writing of the work; each of them read a draft of the entire work and offered copious and valuable comments and suggestions. (Neither of them is in any way responsible for any remaining deficiencies in this work.) Grateful acknowledgement is due to the Sarah Scaife Foundation (and especially to Mr. Richard M. Larry) for its support of the Austrian Economics Program at New York University, under whose research auspices I have written this book. One of the central focal points of our research in this Austrian Economics Program at New York University has been the economic ideas of Ludwig von Mises. I take this opportunity to express my appreciation to my present and former colleagues in this program, Professor Mario J. Rizzo, Dr. David Harper, and Professor Peter J. Boettke (now continuing his prolific research in these same areas at George Mason University), and to those many others who, over the past quarter century, have made distinguished contributions to the revitalized interest in Misesian economics.

Ordinarily, when a scientist's career has ended, his work tends to lose its immediacy; it tends, as it were, to move aside, giving way to the subsequent contributions of others to his discipline. But, as the decades have slipped by since Mises' death in 1973, my own appreciation for his economic insights and understanding has only continued to mature. My recognition of Mises' scientific contributions, and my moral regard for the intellectual courage and integrity with which he carried on his work, have made this project a particularly rewarding one. I can only hope that my little book can help communicate to a new generation of readers some of that same scientific recognition and some of that same moral regard.

ISRAEL M. KIRZNER
September 2000

CHAPTER ONE

LUDWIG VON MISES, 1881–1973

THE PURPOSE OF this short work is to provide a picture of Ludwig von Mises, the economist and social thinker. Such a picture must consist primarily of lines and brush strokes representing Mises' ideas, and explaining how these ideas differed importantly from those of his contemporaries. The subsequent chapters offer such accounts and explanations. But a picture consists of more than lines and strokes; it includes the canvas upon which these are imposed. The story of Mises, the intellectual and the scholar, cannot be appreciated unless it also includes brief attention to the human and historical context within which Mises' intellectual contributions emerged. This chapter seeks to give a brief survey of this human and historical context, a survey that will be brief not only because of space limitations, but also because many of the details of Mises' life, interesting though they may be for a full-length biography, are not, in fact, directly relevant to an appreciation of his intellectual stature.[1] I include in this chapter only those salient features of his biography (and of its historical background) which seem necessary in order for the development of Mises' economic and social ideas to be rendered coherent and understandable.

Vienna: The Early Years

Ludwig von Mises was born on September 29, 1881, in the city of Lemberg in the Austro-Hungarian empire. His mother was Adele (Landau) von Mises; his father, Arthur Edler von Mises, a construction engineer in government service to the Ministry of Railroads, died at the age of forty-six (after a gall bladder operation) when Ludwig was a twenty-two-year-old university student. (Ludwig's only sibling to survive into adulthood was his younger brother Richard, who was to become a noted mathematician, Harvard professor, and probability theorist.) Although his birthplace was hundreds of miles away from the imperial capital, Mises was to spend some forty years of his life in Vienna. From the age of eleven he spent about eight years attending the Academic Gymnasium in Vienna, after which he became a student in the Faculty of Law and Political Sciences at the University of Vienna. With an interruption of about one year's military service (at the conclusion of which he received his commission as lieutenant in a reserve artillery regiment), Mises spent about five years at the university, winning high

university honors in the areas of juridical studies, social sciences, and history of law, and being awarded the degree of
Doctor of Laws in 1906.

The bulk of Mises' work in economics up to this time was
under the influence of teachers imbued directly or indirectly
with the ideas of the German Historical School (about which
more will be said in subsequent chapters), and Mises had, by
the time he received his doctorate, already published several
scholarly works in historical economics research. Mises was,
however, already beginning to rebel against the methodological
and ideological tenets of that school, presumably partly as a
result of his reading Carl Menger's *Grundsätze* at the end of
1903[2]—an experience which, he later described, made an "economist" of him (NR, 33). It was apparently after receiving his doctorate that Mises came under the powerful personal influence
of Eugen von Böhm-Bawerk (who, after retiring from prestigious service as Minister of Finance of the Austro-Hungarian
empire, began to conduct his famous seminar at the University
of Vienna in 1905.)[3] Mises attended Böhm-Bawerk's seminar for
a number of years until he was himself admitted to the (unsala-
ried) rank of privatdozent, permitting him to lecture at the
university, in 1913. It was during this period that his own systematic understanding of economics developed, along the lines
pioneered by Menger (with whom he had extensive personal
discussions (NR, 35) and Böhm-Bawerk, culminating in Mises'

own pathbreaking 1912 work on monetary theory. This book established Mises as an important economic theorist in his own right, and was the foundation of his subsequent fame as a leading exponent of the "Austrian School."

After several years of engagement in various professional economic responsibilities, Mises obtained a position in 1909 at the Austrian Chamber of Commerce (a quasi-governmental body directly concerned with national commercial and industrial policy). It was his work in this capacity which, especially after the end of World War I, thrust Mises squarely into the controversial public issues of his time and brought him into contact with many of the leading Austrian political, industrial, and financial personalities. Mises' career as economist thus developed, from the very beginning, as one combining academic research and university teaching with the very practical work of an economic public policy specialist at the center of ferocious political and policy debates.

The state of academic economics in Austria (and the rest of the continent) will be outlined in the chapter following this one. And it is not difficult to recognize the obvious relevance of Mises' earlier work in monetary economics for the public policy issues which reached the crisis point in the hyperinflations of the early twenties. Here we simply note the fact that Mises' early years as doctoral student, university lecturer, and public policy economist were years of social and political change and turmoil. The old courtly world of Imperial Vienna, center of the vast but crumbling Austro-Hungarian Empire, was giving way to a postwar milieu in which entirely new economic and political winds were to blow with an unprecedented ferocity.

Mises was himself, in his old age, to write about the political and ideological currents already at work in continental Europe around the turn of the century. There is no doubt that the views he expressed reflect his youthful impressions of the social context within which his lifelong convictions were forged. Mises saw the controversies that raged between the dominant German intellectuals in social science and the Austrian economists led by Menger, and subsequently Böhm-Bawerk, as having a significance extending far beyond the substance or methodology of economic theory. Most of the German professors, Mises wrote, "more or less eagerly made propaganda in their writings and in their courses for the policies of the Imperial Government: authoritarian conservatism, *Sozialpolitik,* protectionism, huge armaments, and aggressive nationalism" (HSAS, 23 f). Mises saw the Mengerian School as the champion of liberalism, as the last intellectual source of hope for the preservation of freedom and civilization in the face of the dangers posed by statism and by Marxism. From his perspective at the outset of the last third of the twentieth century, Mises saw, in fact, a "straight line that leads from the work of the Historical School to Nazism," from "Schmoller's glorification of the

Hohenzollern Electors and Kings, to Sombart's canonization of Adolf Hitler" (HSAS, 33-34). In memoirs written several decades earlier (1940), Mises also traced the cataclysmic twentieth-century events for which Marxism and Nazism have been responsible to the teachings of the German Historical School. He reports that Menger had (apparently well before the turn of the century) foreseen that the policies pursued by the European powers would "lead to a horrible war that will end with gruesome revolutions, with the extinction of European culture and the destruction of prosperity of all nations" (NR, 35). It was in this charged ideological atmosphere that Mises' own ideas developed and crystallized.

Mises himself experienced the hardships of war. During World War I he saw active service at the front in the Carpathians as a first lieutenant, but after getting typhoid in 1917 he was called back to Vienna to work in the economics division of the Department of War[10] (MYWM, 25 f). It was his work in that capacity, together with his reflections on the political turmoil which was to follow the conclusion of hostilities, which led him to publish his second book, *Nation, Staat und Wirtschaft*, in 1919. (The book was translated into English many years later by Professor Leland Yeager under the title *Nation, State and Economy*). Mises was later to describe that work as "a scientific book with political design. It was an attempt at alienating the affections of the German and Austrian public from National-

Socialist (*Nazi*) ideas which then had no special name, and rec-ommending reconstruction by democratic-liberal policy" (NR, 66). This tone of the work captured the passion which was to characterize Mises' writings throughout his life. He saw the re-sults of his scientific work as enormously significant for practi-cal policy, if a civilized society was to be created and preserved.

Vienna After World War I

During the years immediately following the war's end, Mises' stature as a Viennese intellectual came to be well established. Several aspects of his work during these years contributed to his prominence in the Vienna of the twenties. His 1919 book did not receive extensive attention. But his 1922 work *Die Gemeinwirtschaft* (published in English in 1936 as *Socialism: An Economic and Sociological Analysis*)—a work thoroughly out of step with both the strong political momentum toward socialism in Austria immediately after the war and the generally favorable attitude of intellectuals at that time toward socialism—placed Mises squarely in the eye of the storm of public debate. Expanding on a seminal 1920 article on the pure economics of socialist central planning, Mises laid out in this book not only his now-famous critique of the possibility of socialist economic calculation, but also his extensive economic and sociological critique of socialism in gen-eral. This work made Mises the archenemy of all those who saw Mises' ideal of a liberal (free-market) society as an old-fashioned

reactionary ideology discredited by twentieth-century intellec-
tual-progressive developments.

At the same time, Mises' rapidly expanding responsibilities
at the Chamber of Commerce during these years of postwar
turmoil involved him directly in the central political and policy
issues of the day. Although formally only a staff member at the
Chamber, in fact Mises' influence became national in scope. In
Mises' own words (written some two decades later): "In the
Chamber I created a position for myself.... My position was
incomparably greater than that of any...Austrian who did not
preside over one of the big political parties. I was the economist
of the country" (NR, 73 f). In his memoirs Mises describes how
he persuaded the Marxist Otto Bauer to refrain from installing
a Bolshevist regime in Vienna during the winter of 1918-19 (NR,
18 f). But Mises' success was severely limited. "Supported only
by a few friends I waged a hopeless fight. All I achieved was to
delay the catastrophe. The fact that in the winter of 1918-19
Bolshevism did not take over and that the collapse of industry
and banks did not occur in 1921, but in 1931, was in large part
the result of my efforts" (NR, 74).[4]

It was during these early postwar years that Mises acquired
the reputation of obstinacy and intransigence—character traits
which more friendly observers would later interpret as the expression of Mises' consistency, incorruptibility, and intellectual
(and political) courage.[5] Mises himself recognized and defended

his "intransigence," seeing himself as intransigent only in matters of science. "I always drew a sharp distinction between my
scientific and political activity. In science, compromises are
treason to truth. In politics, compromises are unavoidable.... In
the Austria of the postwar period I was the economic con-
science" (NR, 75).

Mises was able to use his prestige as a specialist in monetary
economics to help stem, to some extent, the threat of disastrous
inflation in Austria during the early twenties. "If it had not
been for our passionate agitation against the continuation of
the deficit and inflation policy, the crown in early 1922 would
have fallen to one-millionth or one-billionth of its gold parity
of 1892.... This catastrophe was avoided.[6]... The Austrian currency did not collapse like the German currency in 1923.... Nevertheless, the country for many years had to suffer from the
destructive consequences of continuous inflation."

Looking back at Mises' activities during these early years of
the twenties, it seems altogether remarkable that, at the same
time as he was involved in such dramatic political and policy
activity, he should have been able to find the time, the patience,
and the peace of mind to write the scholarly works which poured
from his pen. Moreover, Mises maintained his university affiliation during these years, lecturing and leading his university
seminar. In addition he led his own famed *Privatseminar,* which
met every two weeks in his Chamber office. (This seminar, to

which we shall refer again in chapter 2, attracted some of the finest young Viennese intellectuals. Some of these were to become world famous economists, historians, sociologists, or philosophers. They included F. A. Hayek, G. Haberler, F. Machlup, E. Voegelin, Alfred Schutz, Felix Kaufmann.) It is no surprise to read that, at least to his friends, Mises was seen, already in those years, as "the greatest living mind in Austria" (MYWM, 22).

The truth is that, although Mises would have much preferred a full professorship at the university—a position that would have permitted him to engage entirely in research and teaching—this opportunity was consistently denied him. Mises, admitted to the university as lecturer ("Privatdozent") in 1913, received the title of Associate Professor ("ausserordentliche Professor") in 1918, but never did obtain a full university professorship. Hayek tells us that Mises blamed this on anti-Semitism; but in his memoirs Mises makes no mention of any such "explanation." Instead, Mises writes: "I recognized rather early that as a classical liberal a full professorship at a university in German-speaking countries would always be denied me" (NR, 93). "A university professorship was closed to me inasmuch as the universities were searching for interventionists and socialists" (NR, 73). One of Mises' Vienna students, Dr. Fritz Kaufmann, referred to Mises' often being treated, in those years, with hostility. "This hostility was apparently the reason for the fact, otherwise hardly understandable, that he never became a full professor at the Vienna University, which he certainly would have deserved on the basis of his scientific and scholarly importance" (MYWM, 2nd ed., 202). Mises' influence at the university was limited, in particular, by the hostility of Hans Mayer (successor to the full professorship occupied earlier by Mayer's teacher, Friedrich von Wieser), who, at least in Mises' recollection, "occupied his time with...mischievous intrigues against me."

It was in late 1925 that Mises first met Margit Sereny-Herzfeld, whom he was to marry some thirteen years later. She had been widowed several years previously, had earlier pursued a successful career as an actress in Germany, and was the mother of two young children. In her published recollections of her life with Mises, Margit von Mises included several letters which Ludwig von Mises sent to her in the years after they met. Clearly Mises had fallen deeply in love, and in fact proposed marriage to her in 1926. Mrs. Mises explained that soon after their engagement, Mises "grew afraid of marriage, the bond it would mean, the change that children would bring to a quiet home, and the responsibilities that might distract him from his work." "Lu thought of the task he had set himself, the tremendous work that was ahead of him, all the writing he wanted to do." He faced "the choice between his work and duty to his intellectual ideals on the one hand, and a life of love and affection on the other" (MYWM, 27).

The Years in Geneva

In her recollections (which she wrote in order "to reveal Ludwig von Mises as he really was: a great thinker, a great scholar, a great teacher—but still a lonely man with a great need for love and affection" [MYWM, 7]), Margit vividly describes the tense years in Vienna both prior and subsequent to the almost cataclysmic 1931 bankruptcy of the Credit Anstalt (a crash and the consequences of which Mises had predicted). She also opens up a window into Mises' human character and personality. These were turbulent years; Hitler's 1933 rise to power in Germany was to fatally endanger the independence of Austria.[8] Mises was fully aware of the near inevitability of an eventual Nazi takeover. He had no illusions concerning the danger to his own safety. And indeed, later, on the very night in 1938 when the Germans marched into Vienna, they entered the apartment where Mises had lived with his mother and drove away with his library, writings, and documents in thirty-eight cases (MYWM, 35). No doubt this awareness was partly the explanation for the circumstance that, when in 1934 he was offered an opportunity to join the faculty of the Graduate Institute of International Studies in Geneva, Switzerland, he immediately accepted the offer. His departure for Geneva in October 1934 ended a major chapter (or several chapters) in his life and career, but was to open an entirely new series. By all accounts Mises' six years at the "Institut" (as he often referred to it) in Geneva brought him satisfaction and peace. "For me," he would write in his memoirs, "it was a liberation to be removed from the political tasks I could not have escaped in Vienna.... Finally, I could devote myself completely and almost exclusively to scientific problems" (NR, 137). In his preface to *Human Action* (1949), Mises would describe the "serene atmosphere of this seat of learning," in which he was able to write a major treatise on economics. It is not difficult to understand why, in Margit von Mises' assessment, "[he] never had been so happy as he was in Geneva" (MYWM, 54).

And it was in Geneva in 1938, twelve years after first proposing marriage to her, that Ludwig von Mises married Margit Sereny-Herzfeld. The witnesses were Hans Kelsen, famous international legal authority, and Gottfried von Haberler, eminent economist at the League of Nations. Mises, whom his friends viewed as the epitome of confirmed bachelorhood,[9] had, after years of hesitation, finally married. If the first fifty-seven years of his life were largely years of loneliness, the last thirty-five were to be years of increasing reliance on the protective, loving care of his Margit. If his earlier hesitations had something to do with the fear that marriage might hamper his scientific work, it seems clear that his later work was to owe a very great debt indeed to the unswerving confidence, unstinting encouragement, and sustaining care with which Margit supported him to the day of his death in 1973. Indeed, Mrs. Mises was to devote her years following Ludwig's death to the publication of his writings (as well as both of their memoirs). Margit was to write that, when they married, she knew that a successful marriage required that her husband's "work should be more important to [her] than anything [she] could do" (MYWM, 45). There is no doubt that it was this conviction which was to sustain Mises for the rest of his life, and beyond.

Mises' Character and Personality

In her memoirs Margit von Mises gives us, if not an impartial picture of her husband and of their marriage, at least a nuanced and remarkably candid view of his character and personality. Ludwig von Mises was a strong man who carefully controlled his emotions, but to Margit his affection was overpowering (MYWM, 44). And his commitment to his responsibilities was impressive. On one occasion in Geneva, he slipped and fell on the ice, hurting himself severely. Despite his injury (which a subsequent x-ray was to reveal as a fracture) and the terrible pain he must have experienced, he proceeded to deliver his scheduled lecture and to direct the following discussion (MYWM, 53 f). Yet during the early years of their marriage (as well as during the Vienna years), Margit reveals, Mises was subject to frightening outbursts of temper. "His temper would flare up, mostly about a small, unimportant happening. He would lose control of himself...when it happened the first few times I was frightened to death." Gradually, she writes, she came to realize that these "terrible attacks" were really "a sign of depression," a hidden dissatisfaction and "the sign of a great, great need for love." These occurrences became less frequent after their marriage and disappeared completely after a few years (MYWM, 44). But that Mises' anger could continue to inspire fear is confirmed by his subsequent relationships with the former students of his Vienna days. Hayek has reported that "Mises was very resentful of any criticism by his pupils[10] and temporarily broke both with Machlup and Haberler because they criticized him."[11] Margit has described the episode in which (during a 1965 Mont Pelerin Society meeting) Machlup provoked his teacher's anger (MYWM, 145 f). And Machlup has himself given an account of the episode, the outcome of which was that "for a number of years [Mises] refused to speak to [me]."[12] After Margit persuaded Ludwig to relent and was able to restore "the same friendly atmosphere that had existed in former years" (MYWM, 146), Machlup nevertheless "strictly avoided ever discussing again any questions of monetary policy with him or in his presence."[13] It is worthy of note that, in later years, several of these same pupils (including especially Machlup, Haberler, and certainly Hayek) consistently displayed remarkable personal loyalty and concern for Mises' well-being—in spite of any resentment that Mises may have at one time or another expressed toward them.

Despite the loyalty of his pupils, Ludwig von Mises was a man who inspired sharply divergent personal assessments. His strong doctrinal positions inspired persons hostile to those positions to see him as intransigent, extreme, and lacking in compassion. As Machlup was to put it several years after Mises' death, "[n]o wonder...that interventionists, monetary expansionists, socialists, egalitarians, and laborites disliked Mises, or even detested him."[14] And it was of course precisely Mises' strong doctrinal positions that led those supporting those positions to see him in a brilliantly favorable light. "With an indefatigable enthusiasm, and with courage and faith undaunted, he has never ceased to denounce the fallacious reasons and untruths offered to justify most of our new institutions," wrote one admirer.[15] In addition, however, to the substance of his doctrinal positions, it seems clear that the "intransigence" and passion with which Mises pursued his doctrinal positions (and perhaps the violent temper which Margit von Mises has described for us) contributed to the list of excuses used by those who chose to reject not only his teachings but also Mises as an individual—while his admirers saw only "his poise, his bearing, his European graciousness...his kindness and understanding to graduate students."[16] They marvelled that he had "at his disposal a store of historical culture, the treasures of which are animated and illuminated by a form of humanity and Austrian wit rarely to be found on the surface of this globe."[17]

The First Years in New York

The happiness and serenity of Mises' life in Geneva was sharply interrupted by World War II. Although neutral, Switzerland was not seen as providing any assurance for the safety of Mises, blacklisted by the Nazis, in a European continent overrun by the German armies. When France fell in June of 1940, Mises reluctantly agreed to his wife's insistence that they migrate to the U.S. (MYWM, 54). (Soon after arriving in the U.S., Mises himself wrote, somewhat cryptically, that he left his position at the *Institut* "because [he] could no longer face living in a country that considered [his] presence a political liability and a danger to its security" [MYWM, 138]). In a chapter in her memoirs entitled "Escape from Europe," Margit von Mises has provided us with a fascinating account of the month-long journey—parts of which were fraught with some danger—that took Ludwig and her from Geneva by bus, train, plane, and finally ship through France, Spain, and Portugal until, on August 2, 1940, they landed in the U.S.

Their physical safety was now assured, but this move was clearly a major setback to Ludwig von Mises' career. He was leaving a well-paid faculty position at a prestigious institution of higher learning, in a continent where his name was widely known in both academic and political circles, for a new country where—largely unknown, at an age close to sixty, and without complete familiarity with the language—his chances of resuming a successful academic career must surely have seemed slim. Although Mises entered the U.S. with a non-quota visa based on a hastily arranged invitation to take a six-month position as "lecturer and research associate professor" at the University of California, Berkeley, it seems doubtful if he ever expected that position to offer a permanent opportunity for him (MYWM, 55). In any event, soon after arriving in New York he "decided not to go to Berkeley. He felt that New York was the cultural center of the United States and it was here that he wanted to stay" (MYWM, 64). And, indeed, his first years in the United States were difficult ones, both professionally and financially. A number of Mises' friends from Europe were helpful, and a number of his former students (including Alfred Schutz and Fritz Machlup) did their best to find a suitable academic position for their former mentor, but none such was ever offered to him. Mises gave guest lectures at Columbia, Harvard, and Princeton, but received no serious offers from any prestigious university. And it was not until 1945 that Mises was appointed to a "Visiting" Professorship at what was then a fledgling, hardly top-flight institution, New York University's Graduate School of Business Administration.

Clearly, apart from his age, Mises' unfashionable political and methodological positions in economics rendered him less than welcome in the front tiers of the U.S. economics profession. It would not have been surprising were Mises, after his arrival in the U.S., to have receded into a bitter, penurious old age, nourished only by memories of his former prominence. It is a tribute to his resilience, determination, and personal and intellectual courage that this was not the case. We may perhaps be tempted to raise our eyebrows at Margit von Mises' assertion that the twenty-five years beginning with the year 1943 "were the most productive and creative of [his] life" (MYWM, 89). But it is certainly the case that this period was one during which Mises built for himself a virtually new career, published a remarkable list of books and papers in the English language, won the friendship of a loyal group of new, American supporters, and inspired a number of American academic disciples who would, decades later, successfully spread his ideas to at least a significant minority of the economics profession around the world.

The several years between his arrival in the United States and his appointment at New York University were years of adjustment for Ludwig and Margit. In Margit's words, Mises "missed his work, his books, and his income"; his spirits, she writes, were at a low point (MYWM, 63). A reading of his memoirs (which he wrote during the first months after his arrival in New York) not only confirms this, but also brings to one's attention a certain tone of bitterness toward his academic and political foes of earlier years. Yet Mises did not permit any such antipathy to cloud his dealings with his new surroundings. By his wife's account of those years, Mises plunged vigorously into the New York scene, making new friends and contacting old European acquaintances, colleagues, or students. The West Side of New York's Manhattan was the area where Ludwig von Mises wished to live; its nearness to the theater district and to the New York Public Library meant much to him. A December 1940 grant from the Rockefeller Foundation to the National Bureau of Economic Research (NBER) to support Mises' work initiated an affiliation that was to last until 1945, and this provided a modest source of livelihood.

A small but growing number of American friends and admirers also developed, partly as a result of the enthusiasm and influence of Henry Hazlitt and Lawrence Fertig. Hazlitt was a prominent economic journalist, financial editor of the *New York Times,* who had become enormously impressed by the 1936 English edition of Mises' *Socialism.* This had led him to correspond with Mises in Geneva; he was to be a constant source of support for Mises in the years ahead. Hazlitt arranged for Mises to write a series of articles for the *Times,* and these 1942-3 articles caught the attention of key officers of the National Association of Manufacturers (NAM), leading to a series of assignments for Mises during the subsequent years. Lawrence Fertig had an influential weekly economic column in the *World Telegram;* he often mentioned Mises and his ideas in his columns (and in his frequent television appearances). In addition, beginning in 1952, Fertig was for many years a member of the New York University

Board of Trustees (MYWM, 148). Margit von Mises writes of Hazlitt and Fertig that "they had recognized immediately that Lu was not a man interested in money for himself. So they both did for Lu what he could not do. They made sure that, financially, Lu got ground under his feet again" (MYWM, 90).

Perhaps as a result of his NAM connections, Mises was in 1943 brought into contact with Leonard Read, then General Manager of the Los Angeles Chamber of Commerce. Read was deeply impressed by Mises' strongly held convictions concerning the dangers of government intervention into the free market. In 1945, with the help of a number of influential and wealthy businessmen of vision, Read established the Irvington, New York–based Foundation for Economic Education (FEE). The Foundation's goal was educational, not political. Read and his colleagues wished to communicate the philosophy of free markets to the American public. Soon after its founding, Read made Mises a regular member of the FEE staff. Mises' association with FEE was to be a gratifying part of his work over subsequent decades. By late 1946, therefore, Mises had established himself in his new country, both personally and professionally. And in that year he acquired U.S. citizenship—something he valued greatly (MYWM, 70). He and Margit had, since 1942, occupied a comfortable West Side apartment where his study had a view of the Hudson River. His personal library had arrived from Geneva. He held a visiting professorship at New York

University and a staff position at FEE. These two positions enabled him to maintain both his teaching and his writing activities. Most important of all, perhaps, was that by 1946 he was in fact busy at work on his magnum opus, *Human Action,* the expanded, rewritten English version of the treatise he had published in Geneva in 1940, *Nationalökonomie.*

The 1945-1973 Years

Human Action, published by Yale University Press, crystallized Mises' lifelong contributions to economic understanding. It was a major 889-page statement which systematically surveyed Mises' original ideas concerning economics, economic method, the market process, monetary and business cycle theory, and comparative economic systems (socialism and interventionism as contrasted with the market economy). But the work also included Mises' appreciation for the crucial significance of economic understanding for the preservation of freedom and civilization in human society. It was a work the size and intrinsic importance of which, despite the unpopularity and unfashionability of its positions, did not permit it to be entirely ignored. For those who valued Mises' passionate defense of free markets, the work was to become something of a manifesto. In more general terms, this work was to define Mises' role in the postwar economics profession and his place in postwar American social thought.

The truth is that the dynamics generated by changes in mainstream economics since the thirties, by Mises' migration to the U.S., and by his attempts to reestablish his career in his new surroundings, resulted in his occupying a position in American social discussion which subtly altered his image. During his Geneva years (and, with certain qualifications, also in his Vienna years), Mises was seen primarily as an academic economist whose contributions to the science were recognized, despite their controversial implications for social policy. But by the 1950s, after the publication of *Human Action,* Mises was almost completely ignored by the U.S. economics profession. The dominant changes in economic theorizing and economic methods (characterized by the explosive growth of mathematical economics and econometrics) since 1930—not to speak of changes in economic ideology—made Mises appear, to U.S. economists, thoroughly old-fashioned and out of step, both doctrinally and methodologically. (In subsequent chapters I shall suggest that the economics profession unfortunately failed to understand the economics which Mises was articulating.) The circle of friends and admirers who were attracted to Mises' insights and ideas were, in general, not academicians, but businessmen and professionals in law, medicine, and other fields.

In his New York University classes and seminars, Mises attracted over the years only a small handful of students prepared to follow Misesian scholarship in economic theory as a matter of science (although in the long run those students would make a not insignificant impact on late-twentieth-century perceptions of Austrian Economics.) To the outside world, it appeared, Mises in the 1950s was not only a figure from an earlier era, but one whose ideas catered to the conservative prejudices and practical objectives of business interests. The very unpopularity and unfashionability of Mises' work within the economics "establishment" seemed to reinforce the impression that he had somehow changed the character of his work from contributions to economic science to ideologically charged apologetics for capitalism. The uncritical manner in which some of Mises' admirers fiercely defended his work must have strengthened this impression even further. Moreover, at least some of Mises' supporters probably did see Mises primarily as a social thinker who defended capitalism, rather than as the continuator of the Austrian tradition in pure economics. Indeed, it was during this period that the term "Austrian Economics" came to refer, for many of Mises' supporters, not so much to the subjectivist, Mengerian tradition in pure economics as to "economic argumentation in favor of laissez-faire public policy."

Whether he was or was not fully aware of the way in which he was now perceived, Mises proceeded imperturbably to teach his classes, conduct his seminars, and write his books, as if he was, so to speak, still the respected academician at his Geneva *Institut*. Though he passionately believed in the significance of his eco-

nomics for public policy if a free, prosperous, and civilized society was to be preserved, Mises was utterly convinced that he was
engaged in *wertfrei* (i.e., "value-free," a term to be discussed in
later chapters) economic science. And he offered warm encouragement to his small number of close students, pointing them
toward academic careers and nurturing their efforts at continuing the purely intellectual tradition of Austrian Economics.

Mises' admirers, and his New York University seminar au-
diences, included traditional conservatives who saw Mises' attacks on American liberalism (representing the ideology of interventionism) as making him one of their own. Other admirers
were those who used his critique of excessive government as the
foundation for a more radical intellectual case for pure anarchism. Mises presided over the somewhat uneasy alliance among
his admirers with imperturbable calm. Rejecting anarchism,
Mises embraced conservatism only to the extent that it offered
support for his own staunchly held convictions concerning the
desirability of classical liberalism. Mises articulated this view at
his weekly New York University seminar, where he had not only
students who were formally registered (as part of their work
completing master's degrees in accounting, marketing, management, or finance), but also a number of non-registered regular seminar participants from outside the university.[18] Although
this seminar did not include economists who could reach the
stature of the participants in Mises' Vienna *Privatseminar* of the

1920s, it was from this seminar that Mises' influence toward the late-twentieth-century resurgence of Austrian Economics was to radiate outwards. Murray Rothbard, Hans Sennholz, George Reisman, and the present author, were all, at one time or another, participants in this seminar. Percy Greaves, Bettina Bien (later Bien-Greaves), who were subsequently active in translating, editing, and publishing important portions of Mises' work, were also regular participants for many years (as were a number of others). Yet even at New York University, Mises' academic colleagues did not treat him with the respect that might have been expected for a world-renowned senior scholar. He was viewed as being at least faintly embarrassing to the faculty; sometimes students were steered away from his courses.

In 1956, to mark the fiftieth anniversary of Mises' doctorate from the University of Vienna, a festschrift edited by Mary Sennholz was published in his honor. This volume reflects well the role which Mises had assumed in the United States. The distinguished contributors to the volume included internationally renowned European scholars such as Jacques Rueff, William E. Rappard, Bertrand de Jouvenal, Wilhelm Röpke, Friedrich Hayek, and Fritz Machlup. Younger American economists included F. A. Harper (later the founder of the Institute for Humane Studies, but at that time a staff member of FEE), Murray Rothbard, Louis Spadaro, and William Peterson. The South African scholars William H. Hutt and Ludwig M.

Lachmann contributed to the volume; and the volume also included papers by non-academic friends and admirers such as Leonard Read, Henry Hazlitt, and Percy Greaves. Many of the contributors were members of the Mont Pelerin Society, the international society founded in 1947 by Hayek in order to promote scholarship and inquiry into classical-liberal values and ideas. Mises had been a founding member of the Society (although, as the years went by, he became increasingly disturbed by what he considered to be faulty views expressed at its periodic meetings by some of its newer members).

Clearly, Mises in the mid-1950s, at the age of seventy-five, was a world-renowned figure—even if one celebrated only by a relatively small (but prestigious) band of erstwhile European colleagues and former students, by a similarly small group of younger American economists, and by several other non-academic admirers. When, about fifteen years later, the Institute for Humane Studies published a two-volume festschrift in honor of Mises' ninetieth birthday, the list of contributors was much longer, but the make-up of that list was rather similar to that of the earlier volume. Mises' influence had certainly spread considerably—but it was confined to scholars and others around the world who, whatever their professional distinction in their own fields, did not, for the most part, stand high in the ranks of the professional economists of the time. All this will prove of considerable relevance in the later chapters of this volume, when we consider Mises more narrowly as economic theorist.

Besides his authorship of his massive treatise, *Human Action*, Mises produced a steady stream of books and articles during these American years. These included *Bureaucracy* (1944), *Omnipotent Government* (1944), *Planning for Freedom and Other Essays and Addresses* (1952; this volume includes the important paper, "Profit and Loss," first presented to a Mont Pelerin Society meeting), *The Anti-Capitalist Mentality* (1956), *Theory and History* (1957), and *The Ultimate Foundation of Economic Science: An Essay on Method* (1962). Many of Mises' books (including his major German-language books of the European days) were translated into a number of languages. Mises' influence as perhaps the foremost intellectual defender of pure capitalism spread around the world, and was especially felt in the countries of Central and South America, to a number of which Mises made lecture tours during his American years.

As Mises entered his ninth decade in the early sixties, he could look back on his two decades of life in the U.S. with quiet satisfaction. He had continued to write and publish on the themes he held to be of vital importance to human society; he had seen his influence, while negligible insofar as the mainstream of U.S. academic economics was concerned, spread to a modest but significant degree all over the world. He was still teaching at New York University, and still lecturing and writing for FEE. Indeed, in 1969, even the American Economic Association recognized the lifelong contributions to economic science of Ludwig von Mises, when, a short time before his eighty-eighth birthday, it named him a Distinguished Fellow. And it was on May 29, 1969, that Mises delivered his final seminar presentation at New York University (he kept up his seminars at FEE until 1972, at the age of ninety!) (MYWM, 169). There is every reason to believe that Mises' last years were happy ones. His health, mind, and stamina (apart from a deterioration in his hearing during his later years) were sound until about the last year of his life. The cold treatment which American academia and the professional economics establishment had given to him had never disturbed his equanimity. The honors he received from more friendly quarters during the last decades of his life (including several honorary degrees, a medal of honor from the Austrian government, a 200-guest dinner in honor of his eightieth birthday, and the festschrift in honor of his ninetieth birthday, which included seventy-one contributors) cannot but have contributed to his quiet satisfaction. Margit von Mises reports that after his ninetieth birthday Ludwig "read all the articles that were published about him in magazines and papers all over the world." He told her "The only good thing about being a nonagenarian is that you are able to read your obituaries while you are still alive" (MYWM, 178 f).

Ludwig von Mises died less than two weeks after his ninety-second birthday, on October 10, 1973. His wife Margit devoted the years after his death to publishing (and encouraging the publication of) hitherto unpublished writings of Mises, including his own memoirs (written upon his arrival in the U.S. and therefore covering only his earlier years), as well as her own *My Years with Ludwig von Mises*. In the decades after Mises' death, Bettina Bien-Greaves assembled a massive two-volume bibliography of Mises' writings (including many fascinating excerpts from book reviews concerning those writings), as well as a collection of shorter pieces by Mises. Richard Ebeling also edited a new collection of earlier papers by Mises. A memorial volume marking the hundredth anniversary of Mises' birth was edited by the present author. New editions and translations of Mises' books were published. In the coming chapters we will have the opportunity to define and explore the economic contributions of Ludwig von Mises, and to assess the extent and nature of his long-run impact on twentieth-century economic thought and beyond.

Margit von Mises aptly summed up her husband's character by quoting a passage which Mises himself wrote about Benjamin Anderson (an American twentieth-century economist and financial expert whom Mises much admired). The following excerpts from that passage do indeed precisely fit Mises himself. Both those who admired Mises fiercely, and those who detested the positions which he championed, can agree wholeheartedly that "[h]is most eminent qualities were his inflexible honesty, his unhesitating sincerity.... He never yielded. He always freely enunciated what he considered to be true. If he had been prepared to suppress or only to soften his criticism of popular, but obnoxious policies, the most influential positions and offices would have been offered to him. But he never compromised. This firmness marks him as one of the outstanding characters of this age" (MYWM, 181).

CHAPTER TWO

LUDWIG VON MISES, ECONOMIST

THE PURPOSE of this chapter is to provide an overview of the impact which Ludwig von Mises made on twentieth-century economics. The preceding chapter offered an account of Mises' life, and took note of the political and historical environments in which Mises lived; the present chapter seeks to offer, in broad outline, the story of the economics of Ludwig von Mises in the context of the history of modern economic thought. Subsequent chapters will take up some specific areas of economics to which Mises made contributions; this chapter considers these same contributions—but as making up a forest, rather than as trees, i.e., from a perspective wide enough to permit appreciation for the larger picture of Mises' place in the economics of his time.

The State of Economics at the Outset
of the Twentieth Century

Viewed from the perspective provided by the end of the twentieth century, the state of economics in the year 1900 (when Mises
began his university studies) appears as that of a discipline standing at a critical crossroads in intellectual history. Classical economics—the economics of Ricardo and Mill—had been all but
swept from the stage. In its place a number of contesting schools,
with drastically contrasting sets of methodological and ideological agendas, were vying for professional dominance. The direction which twentieth-century economics would take was certainly not apparent. In fact, not all the candidate-directions
were altogether clearly defined to the economists of that time.

On the continent, the most powerful school of economic
thought was the German Historical School led by Gustav
Schmoller. This school had rejected not only the centrality of
the theoretical method in attaining economic knowledge; it
had also, not coincidentally, rejected the Smithian conclusion
that free markets can be relied upon to achieve the economic
objectives to which, they maintained, "society" does or should
aspire. The work which made up the economics of the Historical School consisted largely of historical and statistical studies
of specific industries, locations, and times, interwoven with
value-laden policy conclusions and prescriptions. To its adher-

ents the work of this school was, unlike that of the "theoretical" school, "scientific" (because it was empirical). But to many observers, and particularly to Menger and his disciples in Vienna, the particular amalgam of science and ideology represented by the German Historical School offered a mix seen as politically disastrous, methodologically suspect, and substantively erroneous.

In Great Britain, the economics of Alfred Marshall was unquestionably dominant. Marshall's economics attempted to retain as much as possible from Ricardo and Mill while recognizing the relevance of the newer theoretical contributions represented by the theory of marginal utility (and its implications). Although most historians of economic thought credit the theory of diminishing marginal utility to the three (independent) pioneers of neoclassical economics—Jevons, Menger, and Walras—Marshall's economics tended to downplay the work of these pioneers, treating the ideas concerning marginal utility as largely his own elaborations and emphases supplied to round out the classical paradigm. The end-product was a body of theory centered around supply-and-demand concepts, which saw prices as determined through a subtle interplay of real (physical) cost elements (*à la* the classics) and purely subjective (marginal utility) elements. It was generally understood that this economics recognized the positive welfare implications of the market system. At the same time, Marshall paid lip service, at least, to the value of the historical work being done in German economics, and was thoroughly open to possibilities of social economic gain to be achieved through appropriate government interventions into otherwise free markets.

A third school of thought competing for professional attention at the turn of the century was the fledgling Walrasian School. The term "school" can be used only loosely in regard to this stream of thought; as of 1900, Walras had in fact not yet produced an identifiable group of adherents. Yet Walras's work represented a recognized approach to economics. Certainly its use of mathematical tools was distinctive. But ultimately its importance lay in its emphasis on the equilibrium construct, and, in particular, on the *general* equilibrium construct. Walras had taken a bird's-eye view of the entire market economy and offered a perspective which explains and accounts for market prices by seeing them as the crucial links in a vast network of smoothly interlocking individual decisions. Although Walras was prepared, on the basis of political value judgments, to sanction significant degrees of government intervention into markets, his general equilibrium system (and that of his subsequent successor at Lausanne, Vilfredo Pareto) tended to support the broad neoclassical presumption in favor of the optimality of the market economy.

Especially on the European continent, Marxian economics was a perennial, if thoroughly unorthodox, contender for men's hearts and minds. By the turn of the century, Marxist thought—

rooted in key classical modes of thinking but steeped in radical and indeed revolutionary contempt for, and intense hostility toward, capitalism—was perhaps the best known among various doctrinal denizens of the "underworld" of economics. The 1893 posthumous publication of the third volume of Marx's *Capital* provoked Böhm-Bawerk, the prominent Austrian economic theorist, to write a highly critical monograph pointing out serious theoretical problems in the Marxist system. This was to initiate (both within and without Böhm-Bawerk's famous University of Vienna seminar after 1905) a vigorous series of polemics pitting Marxist economics against more orthodox theories of value, distribution, and the business cycle.

The fifth (and final) stream of economic thought that we can identify as having existed in the year 1900 was, of course, the Austrian School. The birth of the school is routinely dated as 1871, the year Menger's *Grundsätze* was published. But although this work certainly launched the Austrian tradition, it was not until about a dozen years later, with the publication of significant works by Menger's younger colleagues and followers, Eugen von Böhm-Bawerk and Friedrich von Wieser, that this tradition became substantial enough to warrant being called a school. By the year 1900, the subjectivist economics of Menger, Böhm-Bawerk, and Wieser—an economics offering a predominantly theoretical content to the discipline—was widely known as an alternative not only to the German Historical School, but

also to the economics of Alfred Marshall. The differences between the Mengerian School and the German Historical School
had erupted, after Menger's 1883 pointed critique of the methodology of the latter, into the bitter *Methodenstreit* which raged
during the closing decades of the nineteenth century. This acri-
monious intellectual war, charged with all kinds of heated ideological overtones, largely poisoned the atmosphere of economic
discussion on the continent. Menger and his followers, while
indeed recognized professionally around the world as a distinct
group by the 1890s, were, in terms of numbers and reputation,
overwhelmingly outweighed by the German School. At the
University of Vienna itself economics was by no means
monolithically Mengerian. Several of the professors were in fact
closely identified with the German School. And, as Mises noted
in his 1940 memoirs, it was under the influence of these professors that he entered economic studies.

Mises and Economics: The Early Years

The year 1902 marked the appearance of Mises' first published
work in economics. That work, a history of the 1772 to 1848
developments in the relationship between lord of the manor
and peasant in Galicia (the part of the Austro-Hungarian empire where Mises was born), was, as Mises has explained (NR, 6),
written under Professor Karl Grünberg—himself an adherent
of the Historical School.[1] But Mises has reported that at the

end of the following year, he read Menger's *Grundsätze*. Clearly that work made a most significant impact on Mises. In his own words: "It was the reading of this book that made an 'economist' of me" (NR, 33). We can surmise that Menger's book taught Mises that there exist chains of economic causation that are generated systematically by the human preferences of market participants. No doubt it was this which impelled Mises to become a regular participant in Böhm-Bawerk's seminar in the years after he had been awarded his 1906 doctorate.

Böhm-Bawerk's seminar is famous both for the quality of its participants and the quality of their discussions. Schumpeter, whose first book (1908) created something of a sensation, was prominent among the seminar participants.[2] Others were the pro-Marxist economists Rudolph Hilferding, Otto Bauer, and Nikolai Bukharin. All of these were to make names for themselves in one way or another. It is easy to see why a substantial volume of seminar time was devoted to debates concerning Marxist theory (NR, 39 f). Böhm-Bawerk had, as noted above, published a penetrating critique of central ideas in Marx's value theory, and Hilferding and Bauer were concerned to defend Marx from Böhm-Bawerk's "Austrian" criticisms. It is not surprising that, some years later, Bukharin was to write that "it is well known that the most powerful opponent of Marxism is the Austrian School."[3] And it was, no doubt, his observation of the debates between Böhm-Bawerk and his Marxist challengers that helped lead Mises toward his broader analysis of socialism after the end of World War I.

Although we do not have any systematic records of the topics discussed in Böhm-Bawerk's seminar, they almost certainly included various controversial elements of Böhm-Bawerk's classic theories of capital and interest. No doubt a number of the chapters now collected as volume 3 of *Capital and Interest* emerged as a result of such seminar discussions. In some of these discussions, it seems clear from that volume, several seminar members, such as Schumpeter and Cuhel, stood out. Mises' name does not appear in that volume, but we need not doubt his lively participation in seminar debates. Mises has reported that the last two winter semesters during which he was able to attend the seminar (before he himself began lecturing at the university in 1913) were devoted (one gathers, entirely) to discussion of his own 1912 work, *The Theory of Money and Credit* (the original German title of which was *Theorie des Geldes und der Umlaufsmittel*) (NR, 40). During these discussions significant differences of opinion emerged between Mises and his eminent teacher (NR, 40, 59), and these differences were to be further developed in Mises' later work.[4]

The Theory of Money and Credit

Mises was barely thirty years old when he published this, his first book, *The Theory of Money and Credit*, which was to establish him as an important theorist in the Austrian tradition. Many of the reviews of this book in economic journals were quite negative. But professional opinion regarding the work changed rather rapidly. When Lionel Robbins introduced the 1934 English translation of this volume, he remarked that he knew "few works which convey a more profound impression of the logical unity and the power of modern economic analysis."[5] Especially after the hyperinflations of the early post–World War I years, the book became recognized as a prescient, authoritative work. As Robbins observed in 1934, Mises' book had in "continental circles long been regarded as the standard textbook on the subject."

Mises' work on the economics of money and banking began in a study of both monetary theory and the history of European currencies (NR, 43). In 1907 and 1908 he had published journal articles dealing with Austrian foreign exchange controls and with recent literature on money and banking. In 1909 he had published an English language paper in *Economic Journal* on the foreign exchange policy of the Austro-Hungarian Bank, and a German journal article expanding on the same topic (in Schmoller's "Jahrbuch"). These articles, Mises reported, "generated furious protest among the most powerful members of the Austrian inflation party" (NR, 44). It was in the fall of 1909 that Mises embarked on the writing of his book. Besides having the objective of continuing and systematizing his earlier critical ideas on the practical problems of currency and banking policy, Mises wrote his book in order to reject the then-dominant view that "the theory of money could be clearly separated from the total structure of economic problems" (NR, 56). Mises recognized that in order adequately to complete this latter objective it would be necessary to reexamine and restate the foundations of economic theory in the context of a barter economy. Even at this early stage in his research, Mises saw his work on the theory of money as merely a part of a more comprehensive theoretical undertaking (one that he would in fact complete only many years later). But, Mises later explained, he feared the imminent outbreak of "a great war," and hastened to complete his book, delivering the manuscript to the publisher early in 1912 (NR, 56). He was therefore forced to restrict himself, almost entirely, to "the narrow field of strictly monetary theory," leaving the broader questions of economic theory for later treatment.

Nonetheless, Mises' book did succeed in firmly rooting monetary theory (and, in particular, the theory of the value of money) in more general economic understanding (i.e., by offering an original, marginal-utility-based theory of the value of money.)[6] There can be no doubt of the importance of this aspect of his work for the twentieth-century development of the basic ideas of the Austrian School of Economics. Presumably it was the publication of this book which led to Mises' 1913 admission to the faculty of law at the University of Vienna. And it was in this book that Mises briefly expounded what came later

LUDWIG VON MISES, ECONOMIST   43

to be called the "Austrian" theory of the business cycle—the theory which was, twenty years later, as a result of Hayek's brilliant elaboration of it, to launch the latter's career at the London School of Economics.

Mises and the Economics of Socialism

As we have seen, Mises saw military service at the front in the Carpathians during World War I, and spent the last of the war years in the economics division of the Department of War in Vienna. Yet immediately after returning to civilian life, Mises plunged into his scientific work. Besides his 1919 book (the English title of which would be *Nation, State and Economy*), he published only one year later his famous paper on the economics of socialism, "Die Wirtschaftsrechnung im Sozialistischen Gemeinwesen."

With this paper, Mises initiated the celebrated interwar debate on the possibility of economic calculation. It seems likely that Mises did not see this article as offering any economic insights that were not already well known to the economically literate. He was directing his message at well-meaning proponents of socialism who were ignorant of the basic fundamentals of economic understanding. Nonetheless this article was to play an important role in the development of Mises' own understanding and expositions of economic theory. And it had the eventual effect of making Mises' name as an economist known in far wider professional circles, both in Europe and in the U.K., than might have followed simply from his prominence in the Austrian political economy and financial debates of the immediate postwar years.

Mises followed up his paper on the economics of socialism with a book-length study of socialism in all its dimensions (its subsequent English translation was subtitled "An Economic and Sociological Analysis"). This book, published in 1922, included the virtually verbatim republication (as a chapter) of the earlier paper. It is quite clear that Mises considered the theoretical core of his critique of all forms of socialism (including interventionism) to be the primary argument in his 1920 paper. This argument was that rational central planning is a contradiction in terms—because, without the help of market prices for resources, socialist planners are simply unable to *calculate* economically. Since a socialist economy necessarily lacks a market in which independent agents competitively buy and sell economic resources, such an economy lacks any market *prices* for such resources. But without resource prices, would-be central planners, no matter how diligent and dedicated they may be, are simply unable to assess the extent to which use of a given resource for one specific purpose entails corresponding sacrifices in the myriad alternative lines of production (to which this resource *might* have been alternatively allocated). In other words, planners have no way of calculating the comparative urgency of competing potential uses for any particular unit of a resource. The pattern of resource allocation which the central planners finally adopt cannot, therefore, be considered the outcome of a rational plan. There is no assurance, nor even any systematic likelihood, that this adopted pattern of resource allocation achieves a volume, and a composition, of outputs which the central planners would deem to be preferable to all other possible alternatives.

Mises presented this lesson in economics as his critique of the possibility of socialist planning; it was a lesson implied by and derived from the economic theory of the market economy. What Mises was in effect teaching his readers was an appreciation of the manner in which market prices convey information to decision makers in a capitalist system, permitting their decisions to take mutual account of (and thus to become spontaneously coordinated with) the decisions being made by others. It was this lesson which constituted, for Mises, the core of economic science, and the very fountainhead of all economic understanding. Although Hayek would, a decade and a half later, present his own critique of the socialist economy in somewhat different language, there is every reason to conclude that, in supporting Mises in his critique, Hayek was subscribing to the same core economic understanding that inspired his mentor. In fact, Mises was, in his theoretical critique of socialist planning, laying out his Austrian theory of the market process in a way that would, eventually, clearly differentiate that theory from the mainstream microeconomic understanding of the manner in which the market economy works.

Mises' *Socialism* appeared ten years later in a second, revised edition (1932), and this second edition was translated into English in 1936. It was this later edition which attracted a great deal of attention, both from professional economists and intellectuals more generally. Much of this attention took the form of ideologically based attacks on the work; after all, the thirties were the years in which socialism was widely seen as both the moral and economic hope of the future. Nonetheless, professional economists could not but recognize the cogency of the theory upon which Mises based his critique. In a later chapter we shall see, in particular, how Oskar Lange and Abba P. Lerner, both professional economists with strong sympathies for socialism, attempted to deal with the theoretical challenge with which Mises had confronted them.

The Privatseminar

Besides the impact on the economics profession made by his published works, Mises made a less easily measured—but perhaps ultimately more important—impression on twentieth-century economics through his teaching at the University of Vienna and, separately from his university influence, through his famed *Privatseminar*. Mises had, upon his return from military service at the end of World War I, been promoted (from privatdozent) to the rank of "ausserordentlichen Professor."[7] While this gave him the title of professor, it was not an appointment to a professorial chair.

Nonetheless Mises did lecture at the university and also conducted a well-attended university seminar. But his most important influence was through the *Privatseminar* he held once every two weeks at his office in the Chamber of Commerce. A number of the participants in this seminar have published their reminiscences of it,[8] and Mises himself subsequently wrote about it with obvious pleasure. The seminar had no formal connection with the university. Its members participated by invitation; all were young scholars who had already obtained their doctorates. In Hayek's words, "during the final years of the Austrian School in Austria, it was the center not only for the Austrian School itself, but attracted students from all over the world...."[9] Haberler has described it as one of the important elements of the intellectual life of Vienna during the years between 1920 and 1934. As was noted in chapter 1, the participants included a number of economists who were to become world famous in their profession, including Gottfried Haberler, Friedrich Hayek, Fritz Machlup, Oskar Morgenstern, and Paul Rosenstein-Rodan. But a number of scholars who were to become famous in other disciplines were also regular participants. Among these were Felix Kaufmann, a philosopher; Alfred Schutz, a sociologist; and Eric Voegelin, a philosopher of history. The topics discussed at the seminar ranged widely across the areas of "economic theory, economic policy, sociology or methodology."[10] As Martha Steffy Browne has observed: it is "an important fact which should be reported in future histories of economic thought that the contributions of members to future growth of economic thought was truly remarkable. Many of the seminar members joined the best universities in the U.S. and in England and participated in government projects in the U.S. and in basic work in [international organizations such as the World Bank]."[11]

The work being stimulated by the discussions in the *Privatseminar* of the twenties and early thirties must be appreciated within the broader context of contemporary developments in the Austrian tradition. Besides the circle of scholars that assembled around Mises, a second circle, centered around Hans Mayer, existed at the University of Vienna. Mayer, a disciple of Friedrich Wieser, had assumed (upon the latter's death in 1926) the professorial chair which Wieser had occupied at the University. Although, by all accounts, there was (to say the least!) little cordiality between Mises and Mayer, a number of the participants in the Mises seminar were at the same time members of the Mayer circle. (It was this fact that led Stephan Boehm to refer to the "inter-locking circles" in interwar Vienna economics.)[12] For the most part, it can be argued, the Austrian economics of the 1920s tended to follow up on the work of Böhm-Bawerk and Wieser, rather than that of Menger. As a result, the Austrian economics of the twenties tended to take on a character and offer a substance not at all radically different from what had developed as the broadly shared neoclassical economic consensus emerging from the Marshallian and Walrasian schools. When Lionel Robbins wrote *The Nature and Significance of Economic Science* in 1932, he drew freely from the Austrian writings of the twenties, introducing insights into British economics which had been absent from the Marshallian tradition (and also absent from the economics of Robbins's own teacher, Edwin Cannan). But Robbins made it clear that, in emphasizing Austrian insights concerning methodological individualism, the centrality of allocative, economizing choice, and the related importance of the opportunity cost concept, he was not requiring any revolution in British economics. "I venture to hope," he wrote, "that in one or two instances I have succeeded in giving expository force to certain principles not always clearly stated. But, in the main, my object has been to state, as simply as I could, propositions which are the common property of most modern economics."[13]

When, decades later, Fritz Machlup would attempt to pin down the defining tenets of Austrian economics, the list he offered hardly contained anything to which a mainstream mid-twentieth-century microeconomist might not have subscribed (if perhaps with a somewhat different emphasis).[14] Machlup was, in this respect, simply reflecting the atmosphere of Vienna economics of the twenties. The fact that, decades later, at a time of decline in the reputation of the Austrian tradition, mainstream economists could agree to Machlup's list, merely reflects the extent to which, partly as a result of Robbins's work, Austrian insights had become successfully absorbed into the mainstream. Yet it seems fair to suggest, at the same time, that in spite of the degree of convergence between the Austrian economics of the twenties and the emerging mainstream neoclassical consensus, there were certain signs, even during the twenties and thirties, that Mises would steer Austrian economics onto a path that would eventually diverge sharply from that mainstream neoclassical consensus.

It was during the late twenties and early thirties that Mises wrote the methodological and foundational papers which he assembled in 1933 and published as *Grundprobleme der Nationalökonomie* (much later translated as *Epistemological Problems of Economics* [1960]). And at least some of these papers were, no doubt, discussed at his seminar. It is in these papers (as well as in certain passages in his earlier books of 1912 and 1922) that we find early statements of the positions which would later be systematically laid out in Mises' 1940 treatise, *Nationalökonomie* (and its subsequent expanded English-language counterpart, *Human Action*). These positions include Mises' concept of economics as the "science of human action," the role of a priorism in economic theory, the relation of theory to history, and his views on the limitations of mathematical methods in economics. (As we shall point out in some detail in subsequent chapters, these characteristically Misesian positions would set his work sharply apart from mainstream economics.) So it seems reasonable to assert that much that separates the Mises of *Human Action* from the general perspective of the Austrian economists of a quarter century earlier was in fact being developed, in Mises' thinking, during that very period, and was being discussed in his *Privatseminar.* On the one hand, the Austrian economics of the twenties was responsible for Lionel Robbins's work, which, while it introduced Austrian insights into British economics, was eventually to point that economics toward the standard neoclassical microeconomics of the post–World War II decades.[15] On the other hand, that same Austrian economics of the twenties was inspiring Mises toward a comprehensive revision of the basic foundations of economics, a revision that would eventually render his economics inconsistent with what was to emerge as the mainstream economics paradigm of the second half of the twentieth century. And it was largely these doctrinally radical features of Mises' system that would, in turn, inspire a late-twentieth-century revival of interest in the Austrian tradition.

Mises at the Outset of the Thirties

Mises' place in the economics profession would seem to have become firmly established by the end of the 1920s. He was the author of a number of books, including two major works (*Theory of Money and Credit* and *Socialism*) that would still be in print at the end of the century. His "influence, as teacher and mentor," was, mainly as a result of his *Privatseminar,* "enormous."[16] Nor was this influence confined to his own country. In Rothbard's words: "such were Mises' remarkable qualities as scholar and teacher that...his *Privatseminar* became the outstanding seminar and forum in all of Europe for discussion and research in economics and the social sciences."[17] In a tribute to Mises presented by Hayek in 1956 (in honor of the fiftieth anniversary of Mises' doctorate from the University of Vienna) he referred to the "profound impression" which Mises' *Socialism* had made on those who were young scholars, whether in England, Germany, Austria, or Sweden, during the twenties. That work, Hayek wrote, was on "political economy in the tradition of the great moral philosophers, a Montesquieu or Adam Smith, containing both acute knowledge and profound wisdom. I have little doubt that it will retain the position it has achieved in the history of political ideas. But there can be no doubt whatever about the effect on us who have been in our most impressible age. To none of us...was the world ever the same again. If Röpke stood here, or Robbins, or Ohlin...they would tell you the same story..." (MYWM, 189). By 1930, Mises had published an additional stream of books and monographs, further amplifying his views on such phenomena as inflation, the trade cycle, the ideal of the (classically) liberal society and the dangers of interventionism. Virtually all his later positions on economic theory, economic methodology, and economic policy had been clearly articulated by 1930.

Yet the same Hayek who spoke so glowingly of the international impact of Mises' work on socialism was able to state that, as of 1931, "Mises was still a relatively minor figure confined to a particular field....[B]y the early 1930s, Mises was internationally—so far as he was known at all, which was limited—known to people like Robbins as a man who had done a distinctive contribution to the theory of money, developing Menger and developing most effectively his criticism of socialism."[18] To be sure, this statement was an oral, off-the-cuff response to a rather persistent interviewer (and the statement continues, in fact, to include several inaccuracies concerning dates of later works of Mises). Yet the view expressed should not be declared flatly inconsistent with the more flattering view of Mises' influence expressed in Hayek's tribute quoted above. The simple truth is that, for all his renown in the German-speaking (and German-reading) segment of the economics profession, Mises' books and papers were virtually unknown to the vast majority of the international profession, for whom the only language of relevance was English. It was only in the thirties that, as a result of the initiatives of Lionel Robbins, the two major books of Mises were translated into English. These translations would establish Mises as an internationally known theorist in the U.K. (and, to a lesser extent, in the U.S.), perhaps with the help of the circumstance that he was known as the mentor of Friedrich Hayek, whose star rose phenomenally in British economics during the early thirties.[19]

It may be suggested that there was a special factor that was to help establish the prominent, international professional reputation that Mises had acquired by the end of the thirties in the economics profession. This factor was the widespread recognition by 1940 that Mises' views on economic method and economic policy, as well as on economic theory itself, were thoroughly out of step with the new ideas that were then asserting themselves. Distinctiveness, for better or for worse, helps promote recognition. Although most of Mises' later positions had already been clearly articulated, at least in the German language, before 1930 (and certainly by 1933), these positions were not yet seen, either by Mises or by others, as setting Mises apart from his contemporaries. Mises' distinctiveness had *not* yet been firmly established by 1930. In fact it was in 1932 that Mises referred approvingly to a statement by Oskar Morgenstern that the major contemporary schools of economic thought, "the Austrian and the Anglo-American Schools and School of Lausanne...differ only in their mode of expressing the same fundamental idea and that they are divided more by their terminologies and by peculiarities of presentation than by the substance of their teachings" (EP, 214).

Mises himself was clearly not yet aware of how thoroughly his own views on the method and substance of economic theory differed from what was to emerge as the new mainstream consensus. Quite apart from the extraordinary influence which John Maynard Keynes was to exercise on the profession toward the end of the decade, those years of "High Theory" (as Shackle has called the thirties) placed mainstream price theory on a path pointing dramatically away from the direction that Mises was, more and more emphatically, to take in the years ahead. By 1930 the stage was set, as it were, for Mises to emerge with all the unique methodological and substantive distinctiveness that was to render him so unfashionable and so unpopular a figure in the post–World War II economics profession. It will be these elements of methodological and substantive distinctiveness that will occupy us during much of the rest of this book.

The Years of High Theory

A number of major developments in the method and substance of mainstream economics were to occur during the thirties. The growing communication of ideas in economics across national and linguistic barriers was drawing the followers of the major schools closer to one another and dissolving their distinctiveness. The growing emphasis on the use of mathematical tools in economics had the effect of crystallizing the centrality of the equilibrium concept in economics. This, in turn, tended to promote an understanding of the broad neoclassical teachings that had been common to the different schools, in terms of the perfectly competitive model.[20] (This tendency was encouraged rather than weakened by the emergence of the doctrines of monopolistic and/or imperfect competition.) At the same time as these developments were occurring in the substance and method of mainstream theory, the profession was also undergoing something of a revolution in regard to the role of descriptive and applied economic theory. The emergence of econometrics (and the fashionability of the then-current epistemological doctrines of positivism)[21] tended to push the practice of economics further in directions uncongenial to those who, like Mises, saw the role of descriptive economics as emphatically secondary to the pure, universal truths of economic theory. And of course, the revolutionary impact of Keynesian theory, challenging as it did the relevance, if not the entire validity, of conventional neoclassical economics, was simply one more fatal and painful blow to the illusion which Mises may have had that his own economics was in fact close to the professionally shared consensus view of enlightened modern economists.

By the end of the thirties there could no longer be any doubt: Mises *was* thoroughly out of step with the brilliant, newly emerging economists of the thirties who were, each in his or her own way, remaking twentieth-century economics. Mises differed from his contemporaries both methodologically and substantively. Above all, he was, and was perceived to be, drastically out of step ideologically with the ethos reflected in the new varieties of economics. From the outset of World War II until his death, Mises would both be and feel isolated from the mainstream orthodoxy of his profession. It is of course true that for most of his career, Mises had been a voice representing unpopular economic policies, but for some time he could validly believe that he was representing, to relatively ignorant politicians and laymen, the settled doctrines emerging from "modern economics." After the end of the thirties, Mises was criticizing policies and doctrines espoused and championed by what, in the economics profession, were considered its most outstanding (and most "modern") theorists and practitioners.

It is a tribute to his intellectual integrity that Mises was, in the decades ahead, never to swerve from what he was convinced was the truth, no matter how unpopular that truth might be both in the public and the professional arenas. Quite apart from his ideological commitment to classically liberal principles, Mises believed that the newer approaches did not appreciate the subtler nuances in the earlier neoclassical (and especially the Mengerian and Böhm-Bawerkian) orthodoxy. From this point on he would devote himself to deepening, and making more explicit, the foundations of this now unfashionable orthodoxy. His professional isolation was rendered all the more pronounced by the circumstance that it was precisely at this time, the start of the forties, that Mises migrated to the U.S. His lack of an academic position, his newness to the American professional scene, and his relative obscurity within that profession, cannot but have deepened his own sense of professional and intellectual isolation.

At the same time it seems fair to conclude, from a consideration of Mises' writings during the mid-thirties and onwards, that he seems to have failed to recognize the importance of the new work in economics being done during the thirties. While he of course recognized that the dominant economic doctrines were changing from those which represented for him the accepted conclusions of economic science, he apparently did not consider these newer doctrines as deserving careful, direct criticism. When Frank Knight wrote his review article on Mises' 1940 major treatise, *Nationalökonomie,* he correctly observed that the work "is highly controversial in substance and in tone, though the argument is directed toward positions, with very little debate or *Auseinandersetzung* with named authors."[22] It was as if Mises felt that if he could lay out his own view of economics, with sufficient care to its fundamentals, the newer work would be seen to be simply inadequate and unacceptable, without any need for detailed critiques.

The unfortunate result of this was that in the intellectual environment of postwar economics, Mises was seen not only as old-fashioned and out of step with modern developments, but as being in fact quite ignorant of these developments. This writer vividly recalls an oral remark made in the mid-fifties by a prominent U.S. economist (who happened to *agree* with Mises' policy positions on many issues): Mises, he remarked, had not had a new idea in twenty years. Mises, it was generally believed, had not advanced beyond the economics of the early thirties.

But this dismissive judgment was not only unfairly harsh; it is also demonstrably false. In his 1940 treatise, and especially in its 1949 English-language, substantially revised version (*Human Action*), Mises presented the orthodox Austrian ideas in a manner which constituted an almost dramatically fresh statement of that orthodoxy. Making good use of his years of peaceful concentration in Geneva, Mises was able to follow up his 1933 collection of methodological essays by constructing a grand, overarching epistemological and conceptual framework within which to present his Austrian orthodoxy as an integral part of a magnificent structure of social understanding. Whether one is or is not in agreement with this system, or with the Austrian orthodoxy which it incorporates, Mises' work offers a highly original and uniquely profound fundamental restatement of his own already well-developed economic doctrines.

Fundamentally, Mises' economics consists of the systematically developed logical implications of his *insights* into the nature of human decision making, and of the dynamics governing the processes of interaction among decisions. The tools of his economics were logical thinking and critical analysis, rather than algebraic or geometrical demonstrations. Unlike the newer economics of the thirties, Mises' economics never assessed market outcomes from a perspective of imagined omniscience, but instead always took into account the manner in which market processes both stimulate and are shaped by the *discoveries* made by imperfectly informed market participants. As we shall see, it is no accident that, in an era in which mainstream economics was led to call for massive arrays of government interventions in markets (in order to correct imagined shortcomings), Mises' economics led him to appreciate even more deeply the virtues of spontaneously inspired market processes.

It is unfortunate that Mises did not see fit to directly and specifically address, critically or otherwise, any of the newer work being done in the thirties. No doubt this failure contributed in some measure to his being professionally snubbed in the postwar years. At the same time Mises' attitude was not, perhaps, an entirely unreasonable one. This newer work was being done by writers ten or twenty years younger than he— writers who, in his opinion, brilliant though they might be, had simply not understood the true profundity and subtlety of the orthodoxy against which they were rebelling. It is possible that the fact that much of this newer work was being done in England by economists trained in the Marshallian tradition may have contributed to the disregard with which Mises tended to treat them. There seems no doubt that Menger's disciples viewed British neoclassicism with a certain patronizing condescension. Whether or not there was any justification for this attitude, it would, as we have noticed, cost Mises dearly in terms of post-war reputation.

Mises After World War II

At the end of World War II, Mises was approaching his mid-sixties, an age which (at least at that time in the U.S.) was normally associated with professional retirement. Yet Mises was to continue for almost another quarter of a century to publish works in economics.

We have already noted in the preceding chapter that Mrs. Mises was to describe these years as "the most productive and creative of [his] life." Without accepting this overly expansive description, we must indeed recognize the importance of these years in the overall scientific contributions of Mises. Despite the professional isolation that was to characterize his postwar intellectual work, despite his being (unfairly) perceived as having somehow wandered from the path of the academic to that of the ideologically motivated apologist for capitalism, Mises in fact continued to pursue his own scientific agenda. And it would be precisely the work which he published in these postwar years, and his teaching and seminars at New York University, which would, in the fullness of time, eventually bear fruit in terms of long-term influence over the course of ideas.

We have noticed in the preceding chapter that Mises' magnum opus, his 1949 *Human Action,* was a work the sheer size
and comprehensiveness of which did not permit it to be entirely ignored, even by a profession which considered Mises an
old-fashioned relic of premodern economics. Without fully com-
prehending its scientific contribution, and while emphatically
rejecting its policy pronouncements, the profession could yet
sense the grandeur of Mises' structure of thought, and the ex-
quisite consistency of its systematically constructed edifice. Yet
the truth is that this work was much more than a treatise based
on Mises' earlier work; it constituted a most significant advance
in the economics of the Austrian tradition. This was not simply
a comprehensive treatise in which Mises assembled and synthe-
sized the many individual methodological and substantive contributions contained in his earlier writings. *Human Action* articulated an entirely fresh restatement of the foundations of
Austrian economics in a manner that most definitively and with
commanding clarity set that economics apart from the economic
thought which had, by mid-century, swept the mainstream stage.
It was most unfortunate that the profession failed to recognize
this central element in *Human Action.* The profession missed
entirely the subtle and consistent manner in which Mises presented his unique concept of purposeful human action in an
open-ended world fraught with uncertainty, giving a reworking

of the entire corpus of that early-twentieth-century neoclassical economics which *had* achieved professional consensus.

There is a certain drama in the circumstance that Mises offered this new articulation of the Mengerian legacy at a time when the Austrian tradition in economics appeared to have come to an end. By the end of the thirties, with the dispersal of the economists who made up the Mises circle in Vienna, and with the triumph of Keynesian economics in the years after 1936, the view in the economics profession was that what was valid in the Austrian tradition had been absorbed into the mainstream, and that what was not so absorbed was no longer to be held in high regard. In any event, it appeared that there simply *was* no longer any active Austrian school. When Mises published his *Human Action* in 1949 the profession considered it as perhaps the last gasp of a moribund tradition; it certainly failed to recognize it as a seminal, original work that for perhaps the first time spelled out with clarity and vigor the distinctive aspects of the Austrian tradition. This was a book which would, despite its unfashionability, eventually make its mark upon late-twentieth-century economic thought, bearing much of the responsibility for the late-century revival of the Austrian tradition.

After the publication of *Human Action,* Mises continued to write and publish. In 1951 he published "Profit and Loss." This paper presented features of Mises' theory of the entrepreneurial market process even more clearly than did *Human Action.* This was followed by two shorter books on themes that obviously fascinated Mises. In 1956 he published *The Anti-Capitalist Mentality,* a work in which Mises suggested sociological/psychological explanations for the puzzle (as it seemed to him) of why so wonderful a system as capitalism is so vilified, especially by intellectuals. If this work contained less of what can be described as strictly economic-scientific, his next work, *Theory and History* (1957), offered an austerely scientific treatment of the relationship between economic theory and history. This work builds on the methodological foundations laid carefully and extensively in *Human Action;* it develops themes already initiated in Mises' 1933 *Grundprobleme der Nationalökonomie* (a work which was in fact published in English translation in 1960). Mises published yet a further work on the methodological foundations of economics in 1962 (when he was already eighty years old), *The Ultimate Foundation of Economic Science: An Essay on Method.* And in 1969 he published a revealing and important forty-five-page monograph entitled *The Historical Setting of the Austrian School of Economics,* the English version of a work which had been published several years previously in a Spanish translation.

But the listing of these books does not fully reflect the activity with which Mises was writing and publishing. In the years between 1950 and 1970 Mises published many dozens of shorter articles in English and German (with many being translated into a number of other languages.) Although it is true that these pieces were usually applied economics written for the intelligent layman, rather than for the economic specialist, they attest to Mises' alert and active professional work during these decades. Many of these shorter articles were assembled as books and published after Mises' death.

Ludwig Von Mises and Twentieth-Century Economics: A Retrospective Assessment

We shall, in the chapters ahead, be devoting attention to each of the areas in which Mises made significant contributions. In this chapter we have provided an outline or overview of his life's work as an economist. In concluding this chapter it is appropriate that we attempt to sum up that life's work and contrast it with the course that mainstream economics has taken during the twentieth century.

At the outset of this chapter we set forth the various schools of thought that were prominent in the economic profession at the start of the twentieth century. Mises' first works as an economic theorist were contributions to mainstream neoclassical economics as it was broadly understood and practiced at that time both on the continent and in the U.K. His work constituted a continuation of the Austrian tradition pioneered by Menger and Böhm-Bawerk. While some of the policy prescriptions that Mises drew from his theoretical work were certainly unfashionable at the time, it would be fair to describe the overall character of his work as original, yet solidly within the mainstream of contemporary professional theorizing.

But during the concluding decades of Mises' career his work was thoroughly at odds with mainstream economics, not only in substance and methodology, but in terms of policy implications. Mises' work had led him steadily in one direction—the direction which he saw as implicit in the Menger-Böhm-Bawerk tradition; mainstream economics, which had appeared so congenial to the Austrian tradition at the start of the century, had taken an entirely different direction. The years in which these crucial, diverging steps were taken—by Mises on the one hand, and by mainstream economists on the other—were primarily the decades between 1920 and 1950.

During these decades, which encompass the remarkably vigorous doctrinal developments of the interwar years, mainstream economics took a turn that led it to prize technical mathematical technique over conceptual clarity and depth, to value empirical predictability over theoretical "Verstehen," to rank the reliability of well-intentioned proactive and regulatory government economic policy ahead of that of the regularities to be expected from the free market's spontaneous invisible hand. It was precisely in these decades during which Mises completed his own system, a system consistently broadening the applicability of the principles laid down by Menger and Böhm-Bawerk and consistently deepening their epistemological foundations.

The economic system that he articulated during those decades offered a comprehensive view of the capitalist system, a view which differed in just about every conceivable respect from the view provided by the mainstream economics which dominated the immediate postwar economics profession. As a result, Mises' work in economics during the concluding decades of his career was seen by the profession at large as obscurantist doctrine, evidence of an obstinate refusal to accept the advances achieved by economics in its most fruitful years.

It is noteworthy that, when the century ended more than a quarter century after Mises' death, the perception in the economics profession concerning his economics had changed to a significant, if modest, degree. While Mises' methodological position was still treated as unacceptable, his substantive doctrinal positions, as well as his practical policy recommendations, had come to be treated with far more respect and interest than they had enjoyed during his own lifetime. The consistency and integrity with which Mises pursued his scientific work, what Jacques Rueff termed his "intransigence,"[23] had, by the close of the twentieth century turned the perception of his work from contemptuously dismissed obscurantism into a respected—if unconventional and even somewhat eccentric—point of view.

Perhaps the central element in Mises' point of view, the element which has recently been successful in capturing the interest of younger economists, is his radical *subjectivism,* the insight that economic phenomena express the way in which economic *agents* see the world. Many years ago, in an oft-quoted passage, Hayek put his finger on this central element. Hayek remarked that "it is probably no exaggeration to say that every important advance in economic theory during the last hundred years was a further step in the consistent application of subjectivism."[24] In a note, Hayek observes that this development of subjectivism "has probably been carried out most consistently by L.v. Mises....Probably all the characteristic features of his theories, from his theory of money (so much ahead of his time in 1912!) to what he calls his *a priorism,* his views about mathematical economics in general and the measurement of economic phenomena in particular, and his criticism of planning all follow...from this central position."[25]

This subjectivist point of view is, in fact, stimulating the curiosity and attention of many younger economists who have found themselves to a greater or lesser degree repelled by what they see as the aridity and unrealism of the mainstream tradition in which the profession is still for the greater part enveloped. It is to this curiosity and attention that we can attribute the resurgence of interest in the Austrian (and in particular to the Misesian) tradition in economics, which has, somewhat surprisingly, occurred in the economics profession during the past two decades.

CHAPTER THREE

THE NATURE OF
ECONOMIC INQUIRY

THE REMAINING CHAPTERS in this book focus more specifically on several key aspects of Mises' economics. We take up
first his strongly held and highly unfashionable ideas on economic method. For Mises this aspect of his work was of the
highest importance. Yet it is in this area of his contributions
that Mises has found fewest followers. The purpose of this
chapter is not to convince the reader of the validity of Mises'
methodological positions. Rather, its purpose is simply to set
forth as clearly as possible what it was that Mises so strongly
believed, why he considered his positions to be so critically
important for the substance of his work in economics, and why
those positions have seemed so strange, not only to mainstream
economists intent on disparaging Misesian economics *in toto,*
but also to economists who have enthusiastically endorsed that
economics.

That Mises believed his methodological views to be of critical importance for his economics is clear not only from his explicit statements (e.g., he doubted "whether it is possible to separate the analysis of epistemological problems from the treatment of the substantive issues of the science concerned"), but also from the volume of attention which he paid to this area, especially in his later years. Of the three full-length new books which Mises published after his 1949 *Human Action,* two dealt primarily with matters of method and epistemology (TH and UFES). In addition, Part 1 of *Human Action,* covering some 140 pages (about one-sixth of the entire book), is devoted entirely to the epistemological foundations of Mises' system. A number of Mises' earlier papers of the twenties and early thirties, collected in his 1933 *Grundprobleme der Nationalökonomie* (and translated much later under the title *Epistemological Problems of Economics*) were early—but remarkably well-articulated—statements of Mises' positions. In addition, several of Mises' very first papers written and published in the U.S. dealt with these same issues.[1]

Indeed, this degree of attention might at first seem quite surprising. After all, Mises, especially during the 1920s, was a very down-to-earth, policy-oriented and applied economist. His work would seem to be sharply removed from that of the pure theorist, and even more sharply removed from that of the philosopher of knowledge concerned with the epistemological foundations of economics. If Mises did focus so much of his attention upon questions of epistemology and method, it is, I shall suggest, because he came to be convinced that the vitally important lessons which economics can teach are likely to be dismissed on methodological grounds by those representing special interests. Again and again during the history of economics over the past two centuries, its results have been rejected by those who either failed to understand, or who refused to understand, the basis upon which those results came to be scientifically established. "Political parties which passionately rejected all the practical conclusions to which the results of economic thought inevitably lead, but were unable to raise any tenable objections against their truth and correctness, shifted the argument to the fields of epistemology and methodology" (TH, 2). Perhaps the most effective way of conveying Mises' views on the epistemology and methodology of economics is to begin by recognizing the *intellectually revolutionary* character which Mises attributed to economics within the range of the scientific disciplines known to man.

The Intellectually Revolutionary Character of Economics

Mises saw the emergence of economic understanding in the eighteenth and early-nineteenth centuries as introducing a genuinely revolutionary new insight into man's understanding of the conditions within which society exists. He expressed this belief in words of striking and almost dramatic directness. "The development of economics...from Cantillon and Hume to Bentham and Ricardo *did more to transform human thinking than any other scientific theory before or since*" (EPE, 3; emphasis supplied). Until the emergence of economic thought in the eighteenth century, it was taken for granted that anyone (or any government) wishing to change features of the social landscape was limited only by the laws of physical nature on the one hand and by the strength of will (and the brute force available to enforce, if needed, that will) on the other. "With good men and strong governments everything was considered feasible" (MMMP, 3). But with the advent of economic science, "Now it was learned that in the social realm too there is something operative which power and force are unable to alter and to which they must adjust themselves if they hope to achieve success, in precisely the same way as they must take into account the laws of nature" (EPE, 3).[2]

Thus, the idea that there exist in society "laws" which operate regardless of the will of the rulers was a genuinely revolutionary idea. "People came to realize with astonishment that human actions were open to investigation from other points of view than that of moral judgment. They were compelled to recognize a regularity which they compared to that with which they were already familiar in the field of the natural sciences" (MMMP, 3 f). Mises would claim that, from the very beginning, the source of the new economic understanding was a mode of inquiry stemming from and unique to the *human* character of the phenomena with which the new discipline was dealing. Attempts to discredit the (often unwelcome) policy implications which flowed from the new understanding therefore tended to take the form of discrediting the mode of inquiry central to this new discipline by insisting on rejecting all modes of inquiry other than those long established in the natural sciences. For Mises, then, correctly identifying and appreciating the appropriate mode of inquiry for the discipline of economics is a task vitally important if the practical usefulness of this discipline is not to be smothered and lost through the epistemological and methodological confusions sown by its enemies. It had, after all, only been by transcending the epistemological model of the natural sciences that the eighteenth-century pioneers had succeeded in revealing the regularities that prevail in the market economy. Unless the legitimacy of (and in fact the strict need for) this methodological approach is acknowledged, the essential contributions of economic science have been, Mises argued, tragically and disastrously jeopardized.

Mises and Methodological Dualism

The bedrock conviction upon which Mises built his epistemological system was the insight that "in spite of the unity of the logical structure of our thought, we are compelled to have recourse to two separate spheres of scientific cognition: the science of nature and the science of human action....We approach the subject matter of the natural sciences from without. The result of our observations is the establishment of functional relations of dependence.... In the sciences of human action, on the other hand, we comprehend phenomena from within. Because we are human beings, we are in a position to grasp the meaning of human action, that is, the meaning that the actor has attached to his action" (EPE, 130). Because "we do not know how external facts—physical and physiological—produce in a human mind definite thoughts and volitions resulting in concrete acts, we have to face an insurmountable *methodological dualism*.... Reason and experience show us two separate realms: the external world of physical, chemical, and physiological phenomena and the internal world of thought, feeling, valuation, and purposeful action. No bridge connects—as far as we can see today—these two spheres" (HA, 18; italics in original).

Mises' insistence on the sharp difference between the epistemological character of the "sciences of human action" and that of the natural sciences is, of course, by no means a radical or "extreme" position. The great American economist Frank H. Knight, the revered progenitor of the Chicago School, emphatically espoused a closely similar point of view.[3] Friedrich A. Hayek wrote an entire book, *The Counter-Revolution of Science: Studies on the Abuse of Reason* (1955) primarily devoted to the criticism of "scientism"—the mechanical and uncritical application of the methods of the natural sciences to the field of the "social sciences." Yet the manner in which Mises pursued and developed his methodological dualism led him to formulate certain methodological and epistemological assertions with which few others have felt entirely comfortable. It seems plausible to suggest that the admittedly extreme character of these latter Misesian positions had much to do with the doctrinal opponents against whom he was, directly or indirectly, doing battle—on behalf of what Mises held to be the settled propositions of economic science. Mises was indeed convinced that these doctrinal opponents must be treated as the intellectual enemies of economics.

The Enemies of Economics
I. The Historicists

The German Historical School dominated continental economics during the last three decades of the nineteenth century. As noted in chapter 2, a bitter methodological controversy erupted between this school, led by Gustav Schmoller, and the small group of Austrian economists following the lead of Carl Menger. The flames generated by this controversy did not die down until well into the twentieth century. For Mises the doctrines propagated by the Historical School constituted a direct denial of those regularities in social phenomena which he believed to be demonstrated by economic reasoning. The roots of this denial, Mises was convinced, were to be found in the school's historicism, its belief that economic knowledge must be sought *primarily* in the specific factual context surrounding the particular situations or episodes being investigated. Such a point of view explained the contemptuous rejection by the school's leading exponents of the claims made by the Austrians regarding the universality of economic law, transcending the particularities of time and space.

What rendered the controversy between the Historical School and the Austrian School particularly fascinating, perhaps, was the circumstance that both schools appreciated the subjective dimension of social phenomena. It was of course Menger who, in almost revolutionary fashion, stood classical economic theory on its head by insisting on the subjective character of economic phenomena and on the primacy of individual choice. But the German Historical School, too, recognized that social phenomena cannot be understood apart from human motives and interests. Late-nineteenth-century German philosophers such as Windelband and Rickert had done battle with those wishing to reconstruct historical scholarship on strictly positive lines (i.e., by rejecting all reference to such non-observables as human purposes). They had pointed out, contra the positivists, that the phenomena with which the social sciences (including history) deal are fundamentally different from the subject matter of the natural sciences. Unlike the latter, social phenomena are characterized by *meaning,* by the human purposefulness from which they arise. Members of the German Historical School recognized the validity of these insights. "Nevertheless," Mises wrote in 1933, Windelband, Rickert, and their followers failed "to conceive of the possibility of universally valid knowledge in the sphere of human action. In their view the domain of social science comprises only history and the historical method. They regarded the findings of economics and historical investigation in the same light as the Historical School" (EPE, 5). In other words, to use Roger Koppl's felicitous phrasing, the "historicists offered subjectivism without science."[4]

From Mises' perspective, the propensity of the German Historical School to deny the universality of the conclusions of economic theory led the school to deny the essential contributions of economics. For Mises, therefore, the statist policies supported by the Historical School (policies at variance with the normative conclusions which can be reasonably derived from standard economic theory) stamped the school as an enemy of economics—despite its recognition of the subjectivist and cultural elements in social and economic phenomena.

For Mises, on the other hand, as for all the Austrian School, the subjectivism of economic theorizing, rigorously and consistently pursued, yields understanding of law-like regularities within economic society. Mises found it essential to emphasize the universality of these regularities, a universality which consigns empirical knowledge of the *specific* situations (which may instantiate such regularities) to a distinctly inferior level of significance. Mises insisted on *both* subjectivism *and* science.

The Enemies of Economics
II. The Positivists

After the end of World War I, Austrian economics did not have to contend seriously with the German Historical School, whose influence had by then drastically declined. But a new group of doctrinal opponents emerged. In fact, these opponents emerged in Vienna itself. They were the logical positivists of the Vienna Circle, led by Otto Neurath, Rudolph Carnap, Moritz Schlick, and others. These writers, being "determined to exorcise metaphysical speculation from scientific theorizing" formulated "strongly empiricist tenets."[5] In economics this campaign took the form of excluding any insights based upon introspection and insisting on "operationalism" in selecting elements of reality for scientific discussion.[6] The extreme empiricism of this approach in effect excluded all subjectivist insights from legitimate discussion—offering a challenge to the very foundations of the Mengerian research program. The positivist position rejected attention to human purposefulness and such concepts as marginal utility, except insofar as they could be held to be manifested in observed regularities (in which case it is the latter observed regularities which become the foundation for subsequent theorizing).

By midcentury the fashionability of positivist epistemology had declined from its earlier prominence in philosophical discussion. Economists, however (always having a tendency to grasp the philosophically fashionable tenets of earlier decades), would continue to pursue the empiricist method with great determination for several decades longer.[7] For Mises, and many others, such positivist economics, closing its eyes to subjectivist insights, meant deliberate refusal to see what is readily visible to the mind's eye. Frank Knight was pungent in his reaction to the positivists' refusal to recognize that realm of reality which is constituted by "interests and motivations." It is true, he wrote, that the existence of this realm cannot be established in a way that can meet the positivist standard of testability. However, if "anyone denies that men have interests...economics and all its works will simply be to such a person what the world of color is to the blind man. But there would be a difference: a man who is physically, ocularly blind may still be rated of normal intelligence and in his right mind."[8] Certainly for Mises, too, the positivists, necessarily blind to what he (agreeing in this case with Knight) considered to be economics "and all its works," were not simply philosophically mistaken but the enemies of economics.

Mises' Methodological Defense

Mises saw the central teachings of economics as constituted by its understanding of the systematic operation of the force of dynamic competition in free markets. The entrepreneurial-competitive market process operates systematically to ensure a tendency toward that allocation of society's resources—and that steady advance in society's awareness of its resource and techno-logical potential—which reflects consumer rankings of prefer-ence and consumer awareness of the expanding possibilities of fulfilling preferences hitherto unattainable. These systematic tendencies make up the so-called "laws" of economics. Awareness of these "laws" on the part of governments can help avoid disastrous policies that might unwittingly run afoul of these systematic tendencies. Yet these "laws" are not easily discernible to the eye of the historian or statistician. The German Historical School, for all its wealth of historical scholarship, failed to observe the systematic operation of these laws. Nor did it seem likely that statistical or econometric analysis (unless, indeed, such analysis itself was based on insights grounded in abstract economic theorizing) would be able to detect the operation of these laws in a manner sufficiently clear as to be able to convince the positivist skeptic. Only abstract economic theorizing, recogniz-ing the nature and operation of human purposefulness, and recognizing the nature and thrust of human entrepreneurial resourcefulness, is able to identify the systematic tendencies which shape the entrepreneurial-competitive market process. Mises believed, therefore, that it was his scientific duty to identify with clarity the epistemological and methodological foundations of economic theory, and to point out the epistemological and methodological fallacies that, in his view, marred the economics which midcentury positivist and other schools of thought were attempting, with great technical virtuosity, to establish as the basis for professional thought.

Mises and the A Priori: The Extremist?

Mises took methodological dualism to its most consistent possible conclusions. Not only do the phenomena of human action pertain to a dimension beyond that which relates to the "external world of physical, chemical, and physiological phenomena": along this dimension of human action the phenomena of the external world play no essential role whatsoever. To be sure, human action is undertaken, for the greater part, to attain objectives that are part of the external world. Moreover, such action is undertaken through the deployment of tools and means which are part of the external world. But our understanding of the systematic consequences of human actions as they interact in the world does not in any way depend on the particularities of these objectives, or on the means deployed toward their attainment. Whether members of society compete in the market for food or for books, whether prospective producers must gain command of ploughs or of the services of violin maestros, the general laws of competition and the manner in which prices are hammered out are the same. Understanding these laws in no way depends on one's specific knowledge of those aspects of the external world that are relevant to the objectives of market participants, or to the tools that they employ in their attempts to achieve these objectives.

The source of our understanding of these laws is our direct awareness of the purposefulness of human action, and of the way in which action is systematically modified by encountering changed arrays of contextual circumstances. This, for Mises, meant that our knowledge of the conclusions of economic theory is a priori. Of course, when it comes to the *application* of these conclusions for the analysis of some specific real world event, such as a natural disaster affecting a source of supply of some important raw material, or a piece of legislation placing a ceiling on a particular price, Mises did not need to be instructed on the relevance of and central role played by empirical facts. But, he would insist, there is a crucial epistemological gulf separating our knowledge of the general laws of economic causation and our knowledge of how those general laws are exemplified in specific situations. It is the former knowledge, Mises insisted, that in no way depends on empirical information.

Mises' insistence on the a priori character of economic science was viewed as rather odd, even by scholars otherwise sympathetic to his views on economics. This insistence was treated by others as nothing less than an outrageous challenge to the very scientific character of economics. In the 1938 words of one prominent economist, an adherent of logical positivism, "a proposition which can never *conceivably* be shown to be true or false...can *never* be of any use to a scientist."[9] In more recent times Mark Blaug has referred (in a passage that has been cited with some frequency) to Mises' "later writings on the foundations of economic science" as being "so cranky and idiosyncratic that we can only wonder that they have been taken seriously by anyone."[10] More moderate disagreement with Mises' position has been expressed by his disciple Fritz Machlup[11] and by Bruce Caldwell.[12] Perhaps the most significant (and perhaps also the least frequently noticed) critic of Mises' "extreme" a priorism was Friedrich A. Hayek.

Hayek is often viewed as a follower of Mises (although he was never his formal student at the University of Vienna). Hayek has himself referred to Mises as the person "from whom...I have probably learnt more than from any other man."[13] And in Hayek's own discussions of methodological issues (particularly in *The Counter-Revolution of Science*) he refers to Mises in terms of considerable praise and demonstrates broad agreement with Mises' central positions. Yet in his famous 1937 paper "Economics and Knowledge," Hayek took pains to dissociate himself from a view of economics which sees it as nothing more than an exercise in pure logic ("the logic of choice").[14] Without mentioning Mises by name, Hayek was clearly, if gently, pointing out to his mentor that the propositions of economic theory "can be turned into propositions which tell us anything about causation in the real world only in so far as we are able to fill those formal propositions with definite statements about how knowledge is acquired and communicated."[23]

In other words, Hayek was arguing that the a priori logic of choice can succeed in describing positions of societal equilibrium, and the conditions that must be fulfilled in such equilibrium states, but that such logical exercises cannot predict, explain, or describe the process of equilibration that might in fact bring about the attainment of any equilibrium state. For insight into the processes of equilibration we require concrete empirical information concerning the acquisition and communication of knowledge. This is so because (as Hayek was at the time of the writing of that paper beginning to recognize and to emphasize) the equilibrium state implies complete relevant mutual information on the part of market participants. Disequilibrium implies gaps in such completeness of information. A process of equilibration must therefore be a process of learning. Pure logic cannot, Hayek was convinced, predict the nature of such learning processes; only empirical knowledge can provide the economist with insight into the processes of learning which must make up any processes of equilibration that do in fact occur.

Now Hayek once expressed to a small group, including this writer, his surprise that, on receiving and reading this 1937 paper, Mises expressed his warm admiration for it. Hayek had, with trepidation it seems, expected Mises to express his sharp displeasure at Hayek's thesis expressing his reservations regarding the pure a priorism of economic theory. Hayek was puzzled that Mises had apparently failed to recognize, in Hayek's diplomatic language, his definite disagreement with Mises' views on a priorism.

I would suggest the following explanation, one that cannot only solve the puzzle that Hayek saw in Mises' reaction to his paper, but can also help us understand why, unlike Hayek, Mises did not believe it necessary to consider empirical research on learning behavior in markets in order to understand market processes of equilibration. Mises really did believe that the same a priori insights which permit us to understand how individuals behave in market situations permit us also to understand—at least at the most general level—those powerful tendencies toward equilibration which markets generate. The key to all this seems to lie in the important distinction that sets apart the foundation concept of *human action* (in Mises' system) from that of allocative, or maximizing, choice (in mainstream neo-classical microeconomics).

Following on Lionel Robbins's 1932 *Nature and Significance of Economic Science,* mainstream microeconomics took as its analytical unit the act of maximizing choice (under the constraint of scarcity). With ends and means taken as given, the

agent—whether consumer, producer, or factory owner—allocates his given means in such a way as to maximize the achievement of his most valued ends. All the explanations and predictions of microeconomic theory (insofar as it is the Logic of
Choice) consist, then, of working out (a) at the level of the
individual, what constrained maximization will imply in terms
of buying, selling, and/or production decisions, and (b) at the
societal level, what sets of prices will permit and inspire all
individuals to carry out their planned maximizing decisions
without disappointment or regret. It is because the individual
decision, as mainstream economics thus understands it, is
based on given knowledge or expectations (and contains no
internal devices for spontaneous revision of such knowledge and
expectations) that mainstream economics is unable to account
for spontaneous processes of equilibration (which, as noted
above, consist in processes of learning). Hayek, working within
such a mainstream, Robbinsian framework (in which decision-
making is conceived within the framework of given and known
arrays of ends and means), thus saw processes of equilibration as
necessarily involving facts of the learning process that must be
recognized as *outside* the realm of economic logic. But Mises,
who had a view of human decision making that differed significantly from that of Robbins, saw things differently.

For Mises, the analytical unit is *not* the act of choice within
a given ends-means framework. For Mises the unit of analysis is

human action, a concept which includes the *identification of the very ends-means framework* within which efficient decision making must be exercised. And it is here that Mises' economics, seen as the science of human action, must itself include understanding of the manner in which human beings become aware of the opportunities for gainful activity. For Mises, the verb "to act" includes not only effective exploitation of all perceived net opportunities for gain, but also the *discovery* of those opportunities. The logic of economics reveals not only what men will do in specific situations of perceived possible gain, but also the circumstance that men will tend to discover opportunities for gain generated by earlier errors by market participants (errors expressed in their failure to perceive existing price differentials). In other words, in explaining the source of profit opportunities in the entrepreneurial errors made at any given moment, economics is, *in that very explanation,* also identifying the scope of the tendency of real-world entrepreneurs to discover and exploit pure profit opportunities. The equilibrating process is seen as implied, in the general sense, in the very notion of human action. To be sure, in order to track the specific path of an equilibrating process more is required than the a priori logic of human action. But to articulate the central theorems of economics (which depend crucially, but only in a most general way, upon equilibrating tendencies) nothing more is needed than the pure logic of human action.

It seems reasonable to see Mises' reaction to Hayek's 1937 paper (a reaction which Hayek found puzzling) as reflecting (a) Mises' (apparently mistaken) belief that Hayek shared Mises' own view of things (as described here above), so that (b) he interpreted Hayek's references to the need for empirical knowledge regarding processes of learning as relating only to the applied level—that is, to the task of identifying which specific path of equilibration is likely to be manifested in the real world under given initial conditions.

Mises and the A Priori: Not So Extreme!

As I have noted, Mises' views on the a priori character of economic theorizing are rooted in the primordial concept of "human action," of human agents being perceived as purposeful individuals who are alert to opportunities that might prove beneficial to them. This writer once asked Mises how a person can know that human beings other than himself are indeed purposeful. How can we know that one is not the only purposeful human agent in existence? How can a priori reasoning generate the knowledge that society is made up of rational, goal-seeking persons? Mises' answer surprised me greatly: it may perhaps soften the image of Ludwig von Mises as an *extreme* a priorist. Mises answered my query by saying, in effect, that we become aware of the existence of other human agents by observation.[16] It is observation that convinces us not to be solipsists. It is observation that convinces us that the human race is a race of rational, purposeful, alert human beings.

If we take this oral response of Mises seriously, it becomes clear that Mises' a priorism must be understood as being rather less extreme than it is often believed to have been. Mises was not maintaining that an isolated economic thinker can explain what occurs in market society without leaving his cell. At the very least he must establish—on the basis of empirical investigation, it turns out—that a market society made up of purposefully acting human beings does in fact exist. Once, however, one has, on the basis of such empirical observation, convinced oneself that society *is* made up of purposeful human agents, one can *then*, in Mises' view, develop through deductive reasoning those chains of economic theorizing (based on introspective understanding of what it *means* to be a purposeful, rational, human being) that make up the core of economics.

Mises and Wertfreiheit: *Only a Superficial Paradox*

For Mises, economics is a science; its pursuit calls for strict adherence to the canons of scientific investigation generally. Among the foremost of these canons, in Mises' judgment, is that of *wertfreiheit.* "[T]he scientific character of [an] investigation," he remarked in 1933 (as if this is a matter that is self-understood) "precludes all standards and judgments of value" (EPE, 36). "What is impermissible...is the obliteration of the boundary between scientific explanation and political value judgment."[26] In this regard Mises was following the path laid down most emphatically by the eminent sociologist Max Weber (who had strongly attacked lapses from *wertfreiheit* in the economics of the German Historical School—despite his own roots in that school).[27] Clearly, Mises believed that a distinct separation of a scholar's economic analysis from his personal judgments of value was *possible* (something which many later philosophers have questioned). He also believed, as had Max Weber, that a genuinely practiced policy of *wertfreiheit* was absolutely *essential* for economists, if their views were to have salutary influence and to command the respect ordinarily accorded to scientific pronouncements. Mises concluded his magnum opus, *Human Action,* with a strong defense of the doctrine of *wertfreiheit* in science generally and in economics in particular. There can be no doubt that for Mises this doctrine was a central pillar in his praxeological system. And here is where the *apparent* paradox in Mises obtrudes.

No one who reads Mises can doubt that he was, even when developing propositions of economic science, writing with enormous *passion.* After several pages in which he carefully articulated the above statement expounding the *wertfreiheit* doctrine, Mises concluded his 885-page treatise with the following stirring sentences: "The body of economic knowledge is an essential element in the structure of human civilization; it is the foundation upon which modern industrialism and all the moral, intellectual and therapeutical achievements of the last centuries have been built. It rests with men whether they will make proper use of the rich treasure with which this knowledge provides them or whether they will leave it unused. But if they fail to take the best advantage of it and disregard its teachings and warnings, they will not annul economics; they will stamp out society and the human race" (HA, 885). Anyone reading these sentences can understand the passion with which Mises fought for what he believed to be economic truth; he believed that the very survival of the human race depends upon the recognition and application of that truth. But at the same time it may seem difficult to reconcile Mises' passionate advocacy of the free economy with his insistence on the value-neutrality of the economist. Even so devoted a disciple of Mises as the late Fritz Machlup apparently found such a reconciliation too difficult to achieve.

In a 1955 review of the English translation of a well-known 1930 (German-language) book by the prominent economist Gunnar Myrdal,[18] Machlup expressed this as follows. Myrdal's book was largely a series of criticisms of economists for injecting political presuppositions and ideals into their supposedly scientific discussions. In this regard, however, Myrdal gave the Austrian School a generally positive assessment. "[I]n Austria, economics has never had direct political aims...."[19] Machlup expressed surprise at this positive assessment. "How did the anti-interventionist writings of the Austrian von Mises escape

Myrdal's attention?"[20] But a more careful reading of Mises should convince us that, at least in principle, there is no inconsistency in Mises' position. Although we will leave a fuller exploration of this issue for chapter 6, we offer here one brief observation that relates especially to the topic of the present chapter.

Certainly, Mises maintained the value-neutrality of economic science itself. Yet he also understood and emphasized that *any* human activity, scientific investigation not excluded, is engaged in under the motivating power of ultimate human values. One may engage in scientific investigation for the sake of fame, for the sake of material success, or for the sake of satisfying one's passion to know the truth. No matter what the motivation may be, the scientific investigation, if indeed it is to be a scientific undertaking, must itself be engaged in a manner detached from any value which may be motivating the investigation. As Mises put it, the "objectivity of bacteriology as a branch of biology is not in the least vitiated by the fact that the researchers in this field regard their task as a struggle against the viruses responsible for conditions harmful to the human organism" (EPE, 36). For Mises, a prime motivation for economic investigation is the goal of promoting the very survival of the human race. This motivation indeed accounts for the passion with which Mises fought for what he considered sound economics. It did not, however, necessarily jeopardize the impartial objectivity with which his investigations themselves were conducted.

CHAPTER FOUR

THE ECONOMICS OF
THE MARKET PROCESS

BY FAR THE LONGEST of the seven sections of Mises' monumen-
tal *Human Action* is part 4, entitled "Catallactics or Economics
of the Market Society." Taking up approximately one half of the
entire work, part 4 covers the entire array of topics that relate to
the economics of a market society, including the role of money
and the phenomenon of the trade cycle. We will take up these
latter topics in chapter 5. In the present chapter, we focus on
Mises' broad understanding of the *market process*. It is this aspect
of Mises' economics which provides the foundation for his entire
system of economics. And it is in this portion of his economics
that Mises differed most importantly and fundamentally from
his neoclassical (as distinct from his Keynesian) contemporaries.
It will be important, therefore, to begin with what came to
appear, during the early decades of the twentieth century, as the
shared neoclassical understanding of the market society.

Neoclassical Economics and
the Market Economy

The various schools of economic theory that flourished around
the turn of the century, and which are generally included under
the broad umbrella of neoclassical economics, came to understand the market economy in a way which is still the core
perspective within modern (non-Austrian) microeconomics.
This perspective came to see the phenomena of the market as the
determinate expression of (a) individual decisions made in
rational, utility-maximizing or profit-maximizing fashion, and
(b) a pattern of *interaction* among these rational, individual
decisions, such that *all* of them can be simultaneously and
successfully executed without disappointment and without
regret. The roots of this perspective can be seen, in principle, in
Menger's *Grundsätze,* as well as in Walras's *Elements.* As Austrian
economics developed in the decade immediately following
World War I, the followers of Menger's tradition indeed tended
to believe that their economics was, at least in substance (as
distinct from the technique of its exposition), not significantly
different from that of the Walrasian tradition.

It was to be the Austrian-influenced work of Lionel Robbins
that, in his 1932 book, would introduce this continental perspective to the British (and thus eventually to the Anglo-American) mainstream. It thus became easy for the Austrians of the

1920s gradually to fall into the habit of seeing their theory of market prices as being primarily the theory of *equilibrium* price. It was the Austrian Ewald Schams whom Lionel Robbins cited as the apparent originator of the term "comparative statics."[1] As neoclassical economics progressed, it indeed became gradually identified as almost exclusively concerned with equilibrium analysis (and especially with the equilibrium economics of the perfectly competitive model—of which more will be discussed later in this chapter.) A concentration on equilibrium tends to divert analytical attention away from the *process* of equilibration. In Frank Machovec's opinion, the course of neoclassical economics during the first four decades of this century indeed saw its transformation from a theory of process to one of (perfectly competitive) equilibrium.[2] Mises never accepted, nor did he play a role in, any such transformation.

Mises and the Market Process

"What distinguishes the Austrian School and will lend it immortal fame is precisely the fact that it created a theory of economic action and not of economic equilibrium or non-action" (NR, 36). Writing this in 1940 (shortly after the publication of his *Nationalökonomie*), Mises recognized that economic thought cannot do without the idea of equilibrium, but maintained that the Austrian School "is always aware of the purely instrumental nature of such an idea" (NR, 36). The core of economic understanding, for Mises, does not consist in the elucidation of the conditions required to be fulfilled in the state of equilibrium; the core of economic understanding consists, instead, in revealing the systematic character of the market process—a process set in motion precisely by the circumstance that the conditions for equilibrium have *not* been fulfilled. "The market," Mises wrote in 1949, "is not a place, a thing, or a collective entity. The market is a *process,* actuated by the interplay of the actions of the various individuals cooperating under the division of labor" (HA, 257; emphasis supplied).

The Entrepreneurial Character of the Misesian Market Process

The prime active element in the Misesian market process is the profit-motivated activity of entrepreneurs. "The driving force of the market, the element tending toward unceasing innovation and improvement, is provided by the restlessness of the promoter and his eagerness to make profits as large as possible" (HA, 255). "The driving force of the market process is provided...by the promoting and speculating entrepreneurs" (HA, 328). The entrepreneur is the person who acts in the face of uncertainty; in the imaginary, settled world of the equilibrium state, without uncertainty, there is no scope for entrepreneurial activity (HA, 252-3). More narrowly, Mises observed, the term "entrepreneur" is used in economics to refer to those "who have more initiative, more venturesomeness, and a quicker eye than the crowd, the pushing and promoting pioneers of economic improvement" (HA, 255). (When Mises uses the word "promoter," he wishes to draw our attention to this narrower subset of the broader category of entrepreneurship.) The entrepreneurial function is the correction of "maladjustments" in market prices and decisions. When an entrepreneur is able to grasp pure profit by buying factors of production at prices below those of the products they generate, he has discovered, and moved to correct, such a maladjustment. The maladjustment consisted in the fact that the factor prices were "from the point of view of the future state of the market...too low."[3] Entrepreneurial profit and loss "are generated by success or failure in adjusting the course of production activities to the most urgent wants of the consumers."[4]

There is, in the Misesian view of things, a one-to-one correspondence between (a) maladjustments in the market, reflecting earlier entrepreneurial "errors" (i.e., failures to anticipate the true conditions of—and the true potential arising out of—resource supply and consumer demand), and (b) opportunities for profit that are likely to alert potential entrepreneurs to act, in the face of the ineradicable uncertainty of the future, in ways consistent with the correction of those maladjustments. The market process, then, consists of continual discoveries (and "corrections") of such maladjustments/pure-profit opportunities by entrepreneurial market participants. These discoveries are being continually pointed in new directions by the never-ceasing flood of exogenous changes (such as autonomous changes in consumer preferences, autonomous changes in resource supply conditions, and autonomous changes in technological possibilities). To see and to describe the continuous market process of entrepreneurial discoveries as *equilibrating* in character is to be both illuminating and possibly misleading at the same time. It is misleading to see this process as equilibrating, not only because the continual flood of exogenous changes render the attainment of equilibrium utterly unthinkable, but also because that flood of change virtually ensures that the direction of innovative entrepreneurial decisions at any given moment is likely *not* to be consistent with the patterns of potential adjustment implicit in the exogenous changes about to occur *after* that given moment.

Yet, at the same time, there *is* an illuminating quality to the Misesian insight that the innovative moves of entrepreneurs within any given period constitute a systematic "corrective" (and thus "equilibrative") series of steps *from the perspective of the entrepreneurial insights of that period.* Those insights have (at least in the judgments of the relevant entrepreneurs) revealed existing "maladjustments" among earlier market decisions; these discoveries have triggered entrepreneurial moves, the effect of which, *absent further unanticipated change,* will be to correct the earlier maladjustments. The insight that the absence of unanticipated

change is itself something *not* to be anticipated does not erase
the valuable character of the insight that, in a well-defined sense,
these discoveries have set in motion equilibrating, corrective,
entrepreneurial adjustments. The valuable character of this insight lies in its illuminating clarification of the definite sense in
which the entrepreneur-driven market process is *not* a free-float-
ing series of random changes, but rather is, at each and every
instant, a process operating under powerful forces which continually produce outcomes that are, if not "determinate" (as
they certainly are not!), at least systematically and benignly inspired by error-correcting incentives. Seen from the Misesian
perspective, the ceaseless agitation of the market becomes "understandable" as the continuous flow of corrective discoveries,
linked to the current and anticipated conditions (of resource
supply, consumer demand, and technological knowledge) by
powerful tendencies of entrepreneurs to discover what it is in
their interest to discover.[5]

The Dynamically Competitive Character of the Misesian Market Process

Although Mises himself did not emphasize this aspect of
his system, the present writer has found it useful to point out
that if the Misesian market process is an entrepreneurial one, it
is, by that very token, also a dynamically *competitive* process.[6]
Mises referred to what he called "catallactic competition" as

being "one of the characteristic features of the market economy" (HA, 272). In this regard Mises had in mind the incentives operating upon competing producers to seek improved ways of serving the consumer. What creates these incentives is the awareness of producers that others are free to enter their "territories" and compete for their customers' allegiance. What is needed in order to ensure freedom of what Mises called "catallactic competition"[7] is simply the absence of artificial barriers to entry that might restrict entrepreneurial entry into a field in which improvements for consumer satisfaction might be held to be possible and worthwhile. The point is that dynamically competitive entry into a market *means* entrepreneurial entry, so that to recognize the entrepreneurial character of the Misesian market process is to recognize its dynamically competitive character.

What we have referred to as *dynamic* competition (and we have used this term as equivalent to Mises' "catallactic" competition) differs, it must be emphasized, from the concept of competition used in mainstream neoclassical textbooks for the past six or seven decades. Mainstream neoclassical textbooks, following especially upon the ideas of Frank H. Knight, have identified competition, in its most "perfect" form, as referring to a particular *equilibrium* or *state of affairs.* In this state of affairs, the imagined universality of information and knowledge, and the imagined extremely large number of market participants, combine with other elements to ensure that, at each and every instant, each potential seller (buyer) is confronted with a perfectly elastic demand (supply) curve. In other words the state of perfect competition is one in which (a) the market price has *already* (before the model of perfect competition has had a chance to "perform") somehow been set at the equilibrium level (and each market participant is too insignificant to be able to make any change in that price), and in which (b) each market participant (correctly) sees himself as able to carry out all his selling (or buying) decisions at the market price without disappointment and without regret. Mises must have found this model of perfect competition not only wildly unrealistic (something never denied by neoclassical economists), but also analytically obfuscating. He seems to have deliberately ignored this model in all his writing on the role of competition in markets.

Thus, while the perfectly competitive state (being an equilibrium situation) cannot possibly provide scope for the Misesian entrepreneur, the dynamically competitive process (in which, for Mises, the consumers assign success and failure among the competing producers) is *essentially* entrepreneurial. An act of competitive entry is necessarily entrepreneurial; it expresses the implicit conviction of the entering competitor that profits can be won by directing some particular resources away from their current destinations toward the production of a particular product, which they expect to be able to sell at a profit. The entrepreneurial market process thus consists of an endless series of entrepreneurial steps, each of which constitutes an act of "entry." The generally understood benign character of "competition" thus consists, in the Misesian perspective, in its permitting and stimulating a continual flow of entrepreneurial ventures. These ventures introduce new products and new methods of production, but they also introduce new prices into the market, for both resources and products. These new prices explore possibilities for attracting resources to where they can be most productive, as judged by consumers; they explore possibilities for making products available to consumers at lower costs to them.

The sense in which Mises believed that consumers are well served by the market process depends on the *competitive* character of this process, that is, on the extent to which the institutions of the market permit and encourage entrepreneurs to enter sectors of the market where they believe they can win profit. For the Misesian market process, "competition" means simply an institutional framework characterized by *freedom of entrepreneurial entry,* or, equivalently, the absence of privileges granted to incumbents, which serve as artificial barriers to entry.

Mises and Mainstream Price Theory

All this adds up to a significant difference between the Misesian understanding of the market process and the mainstream neoclassical theory of competitive price. The latter theory sees prices as emerging spontaneously out of the imagined conditions of perfectly competitive supply and demand. These prices are, at each and every instant, equilibrium prices. The task of the pure theory of price is seen as fully accomplished by the identification of the conditions that must be fulfilled—at the level of the consumer, at the level of the producer, and at the level of the resource owner—in order for all decisions to be able to be carried out simultaneously without disappointment and without regret. From this perspective, this price theory is helpful in understanding the real world because the *predictions* of the model are in fact approximately fulfilled in the real world (even though, it is of course conceded, the real world does *not* exemplify the *assumptions* of the perfectly competitive equilibrium model). In other words, mainstream theory applies its competitive model to the real world by treating that world as having, at each and every moment, attained the equilibrium state. For Mises, the nature and applicability of market process theory is entirely different.

For Mises, the identification of what might be the equilibrium price (given the current state of supply and demand) is of distinctly secondary importance. (Mises at one point refers to the drawing of supply and demand diagrams as possibly helpful for teaching purposes, but as not really helpful in understanding the essential analytics of market price determination

[HA, 333]). What is important for Mises is to understand the dynamic process continually at work in markets, operating to identify where resource or product prices are "too high" or "too low," and operating to "correct" them by attracting appropriate entrepreneurial discoveries.[8] The diagrams which dominate the microeconomics textbooks have virtually no place in the Misesian system. These diagrams identify optimal decisions for various market participants (including, especially, producing firms) under a variety of assumed demand and cost situations. They throw no light on the dynamics through which these relevant demand and cost situations, as they confront the various decision makers, are themselves being changed in the course of the market process.

Where the mainstream theory of price has, because it is an equilibrium theory, squeezed the entrepreneurial role out of existence, Misesian theory places that role at the very center of the analytics of the process.

One very important result of these differences between the Misesian theory of the market process and the mainstream neoclassical theory of price, is that these two approaches have two entirely different perspectives on the meaning and significance of *monopoly* in the working of markets. (As we shall see in a later chapter, a direct implication of these different perspectives is that they generate two entirely contrasting views on the appropriate public policy in regard to the phenomenon of monopoly.)[9]

The Place of Monopoly in the Misesian System
I.

In mainstream neoclassical economics, the idea of monopoly has come to mean a market in which a seller has a certain control over his price, reflected in his being confronted by a demand curve for his product that is less than perfectly elastic (i.e., not horizontal but downward sloping). In such a market the monopolist can, by limiting the quantity he offers for sale, choose his price (whereas in the perfectly competitive market each seller finds the price somehow set automatically by "the market"; he is powerless to sell at any other price.) Mainstream price theory then focuses on the differences that separate the price and output decision of the monopolist from the aggregate price and output outcomes of perfectly competitive industries, and on the evaluation of these differences from the perspective of their social welfare implications. To the extent that a seller is indeed a monopolist, his price is *not* determined by competition, but by his own profit-maximizing calculation.

For Mises, however, the notion of monopoly, as we shall see, is rather different. We can perhaps best grasp this difference by pondering the following statement by Mises: "It would be a serious blunder to deduce from the antithesis between monopoly price and competitive price that the monopoly price is the outgrowth of the absence of competition. There is always catallactic competition on the market. Catallactic competition is no less a factor in the determination of monopoly prices than it is in the determination of competitive prices" (HA, 278). At first glance this seems puzzling. Surely, if monopoly is in some sense the antithesis of competition, competition can hardly be a determining factor in generating monopoly price. The solution to this puzzle lies in Mises' understanding of what competition is (and in his consequently quite unusual definition of what monopoly means).

Mises believed that the dynamic process of entrepreneurial competition is *always* at work in the market. So long as there *is* a market, it necessarily consists, for Mises, in the scope it offers for the dynamic competitive process to proceed. There is, in this dynamic process of competition, nothing to ensure that market participants have no control over price (that they be seen as "price-takers"). On the contrary, a most important dimension along which dynamic competition proceeds is that of price; market participants compete with each other by offering to sell (or buy) at lower (or higher) prices than others. Thus, monopoly cannot be defined in terms of the less-than-perfect elasticity of the demand curve faced by the monopolist. Instead, it must be defined in terms of the obstacles to entry that protect the monopolist from the competition of others. In the absence of governmentally granted monopoly privileges, Mises found only one source of such obstacles to entry to be possible: *the possibility that one seller*

controls the entire supply of a particular scarce resource that is of great
importance to a particular branch of production. The conditions of
competition surrounding this branch of production are now
different from what they would be in the absence of the resource
monopoly. Competition is not absent; the resource monopoly
has forced the competitive process into different channels, as it
were. From the space defined by the scope of the scarce monopolized resource, the force of the competitive process has been
pushed outside, but the process continues to exercise determining power over the monopolist's prices.

It is still this competitive process, and only this competitive
process, which is at work in helping determine the price that the
monopolist producer will select. Just as the competitive process
nudges a competitive producer to select his price (based on his
entrepreneurial judgment concerning his alternative opportunities), so the competitive process nudges the monopolist producer
to select his price in similar fashion. "The shape of the demand
curve that...directs the monopolist's conduct is determined by
the competition of all other commodities competing for the
buyers' dollars.... On the market every commodity competes
with all other commodities" (HA, 278). Now, mainstream theorists would recognize that the monopolist's demand curve is
determined by happenings in other industries. But they would
prefer to say that, *given* the monopolist's demand curve, its very
shape dictates that the manner in which he selects his price is

simply *not* competitive. Mises, on the other hand, alive as he was to the dynamic character of competition, sees the monopolist as at all times engaged in active entrepreneurial competition (with producers in other industries) for the consumer dollar, in a manner not different, in principle, from the manner in which competing producers compete actively in *any* competitive market.

The obvious question which presents itself, then, is precisely how a monopolized industry differs from a competitive industry, in the Misesian view of things. In both kinds of industry, we have seen, each producer-seller exercises *some* degree of control over price. In both kinds of industry, prices are determined, in large part, by the activities of competitors (in the same or in other industries). What positive differences separate the two kinds of industries? Is there any sense in which, for Mises, the monopolized industry can be pronounced economically "bad," or socially "inefficient"? To answer these questions we must first offer a brief digression concerning "consumer sovereignty," and its role in Mises' system of economic thought.

The Doctrine of Consumer Sovereignty

Although the Misesian theory of the competitive market process is a positive one, in that it simply describes and explains what occurs in a free market, the theory does lead indirectly to possible policy implications. For Mises, one possible link between his theory and policy was the concept of consumer sovereignty. In a brief section of *Human Action* (a section entitled "The Sovereignty of the Consumers"), Mises explained this concept. In the market, he argued, while it is the entrepreneur-producers who directly control production and "are at the helm and steer the ship," they are not supreme; the "captain is the consumer" (HA, 270). "A wealthy man can preserve his wealth only by continuing to serve the consumers in the most efficient way." Owners of material factors of production can prosper from the value represented by their assets only by placing those assets at the service of consumers in the ways preferred by consumers. It is by his decisions to buy and to refrain from buying that the consumer controls the pattern of production. The competition of entrepreneurs for profit leads them to seek more and more accurately to anticipate consumer preferences, and to move energetically, efficiently, and imaginatively to seek ways of catering to those preferences. In particular, as long as scarcity governs human society, competition for entrepreneurial profit expresses consumer sovereignty by tending to ensure that every ounce of potential resources is employed to further consumer satisfaction. Consumer sovereignty "forbids" the possibility of idle, wasted resources.

It is reasonable to interpret Mises' emphasis upon the notion of consumer sovereignty as expressing a profoundly Mengerian insight.[10] Menger had pioneered the theory of market prices as governed, both at the product level and at the resource level, by the demand of the consumer. The valuations of consumers (given the configuration of resource availability) determine the values of resources of production. Mises was simply pursuing this insight to its logical conclusion. He pointed out that market outcomes, the allocation of society's resources, are under the ultimate control of consumers. The consumers are sovereign.

Certainly, so stated, this doctrine is a positive one; it is, by itself, *wertfrei*. Whether one is made happy or unhappy by the thought that consumers ultimately dictate the course of production, the *fact* of consumer sovereignty stands. But it is easy to see the implications of this doctrine for public policy in an environment in which public opinion favors consumer supremacy. As we shall see in chapter 6, it is certainly this which underlay much of Mises' lifelong convictions concerning the economic desirability of free markets. For present purposes, however, it is not necessary to proceed beyond the purely positive doctrine of consumer sovereignty. We shall see that it is from the perspective of this doctrine that Mises' views on the consequences of monopoly become clear.

The Place of Monopoly in the Misesian System
II.

We must remember that for Mises the defining feature of the monopolist is his exclusive control over some important scarce resource. Because no one else can produce the product (for which

this resource is a necessary ingredient), the owner of this monopolized resource *may* find it in his own interest to *destroy* part
of his supply of this resource—if doing so would allow him to
raise its price to a level that will maximize the revenue he can
obtain from his resource. This *need* not be the case. It may *not*
be possible to enhance revenue by withholding some of the
resource from production. But where it is the case that the price
of a resource has been raised through the deliberate withholding of supply from the market, Mises used the term "monopoly
price." He saw this case as one which, while certainly possible,
is extremely unlikely and rather unimportant from a practical
point of view. (It is also virtually impossible to establish such a
case empirically, since we are never in a position to know objec-
tively whether the nonutilization of a monopolized resource was
indeed motivated by the objective of enhancing revenue—it
could have been motivated by the monopolist's speculation concerning a future price rise, or by his own desire not to use his
resource for industrial purposes but instead to enjoy it in his
capacity as consumer.)

For Mises, the monopoly price case is a unique situation
ordinarily not able to occur in a market economy. Where a
monopoly price has occurred, this means that the monopoly
owner of the resource has successfully defied the preferences of
consumers. He has been able to extract value from his assets, *not*
by putting them at the service of the consuming public, but, to

the contrary, by withholding them from such service. In the Misesian system such a possibility was fascinating (if unlikely); it meant that the doctrine of consumer sovereignty was, in one possible respect, not universally validated. Where the market economy generally imposes a *harmony* of interests among resource owners and consumers, monopoly resource ownership offers the possibility of a *conflict* of interests.

We should emphasize that, in enunciating this theory of monopoly, Mises was *not* drawing policy conclusions supporting state action against monopolies. His doctrine was stated at the positive level. (Indeed, the Misesian system strongly suggests the inappropriateness of the antitrust policies that Western capitalist countries adopted during the first decades of the twentieth century and earlier.)

For anyone familiar with the mainstream neoclassical theory of monopoly, Mises' theory cannot fail to appear quite strange. But its strangeness arises entirely from the profound differences, noted earlier, that separate the Misesian theory of the market from the mainstream neoclassical theory.[11]

For the mainstream theory, the theory of monopoly begins with a downward sloping demand curve confronting the monopolist producer. With a degree of control thus available to the monopolist producer, he selects the price which maximizes his net gain ("profit," in textbook terminology) by (a) producing a quantity which is lower than would have been produced were this monopolist somehow replaced by a perfectly competitive industry, and (b) charging a price shown to be higher than his marginal cost of production. The uniqueness of monopoly, in the mainstream neoclassical view, lies in these two implications of the downward sloping demand curve facing the monopolist producer.

But for Mises, *every* producer, even under (dynamically) competitive conditions, has a degree of entrepreneurial "control" over price (at least insofar as we can talk of "control" in the face of the radical uncertainty of an open-ended world). The question that Mises would pose for neoclassical theory would be: "what is it that (in the absence of governmentally granted privileges) protects the monopolist's profits from being whittled away by new entrants?" The answer, Mises would say, must lie in an implicitly postulated unique ownership over a scarce resource. The interesting implication for Mises, then, follows in the possibility that such monopoly ownership of a resource may lead to some of its supply being deliberately withheld from satisfaction of consumer preferences. The emphasis is not on the monopolist as producer (possibly, as a result, producing less than might otherwise have been produced), but on the monopolist resource owner, who may be motivated to act along lines that conflict with the interests of the consumer—a possibility never, in the Misesian system, otherwise arising under free market conditions.

The Pricing of Factors of Production

In mainstream neoclassical price theory, the prices of resource services (such as labor and the use of land) are seen as determined in markets which are parallel to the markets for the products which these resources produce. Just as supply and demand determine product prices in competitive markets, so too do supply and demand determine resource prices in competitive markets. Where the market demand curve for products is derived from marginal utility, the market demand curve for resources is derived from marginal productivity. It is this mainstream neoclassical insight that informs the textbook chapters on the so-called "marginal productivity theory of distribution" (largely based on the century-old work of the U.S. economist John Bates Clark). Mises would have, in regard to factor pricing, few new points of disagreement with the mainstream theory beyond those we have discussed with regard to the market process in general. In other words, Mises would of course be impatient with a strictly equilibrium theory of factor prices; and he would be impatient with the notions of perfect competition implicit in much of the mainstream theory. But, subject to the modifications implicit in these objections, he would in principle accept the Clarkian notion of "derived demand."

In this, indeed, Mises would simply be following the route, outlined in Carl Menger's 1871 work, in which the prices of

resources ("higher order goods") are seen as derived by the
market from the prices (themselves the expression of consumer
valuations) of the consumer goods ("goods of lowest order").
Although Mises rarely used the term "marginal productivity"
(HA, 597), he certainly accepted the general neoclassical insight
that the wage which an employer of labor will offer is based on
that employer's assessment of the additional revenue expected
to be forthcoming from the laborer's productive efforts. What
Mises emphasized, possibly more than is the case in mainstream neoclassical theory, is what he somewhat awkwardly
referred to as the "connexity of prices" (HA, 391 f). Following on
Menger's insights concerning the linkages between the markets
and prices of higher order goods and those of lower order goods,
Mises saw the panorama of prices (of all resources and of all
products) as linked in a dynamic competitive market process.
Because one factor—labor—is necessary for every kind of production, and because in general the efforts of a laborer can be
directed to a variety of different kinds of output, the connexity
of prices emerges. It is this which "integrates the pricing into a
whole in which all gears work on one another. It makes the
market a concatenation of mutually interdependent phenomena" (HA, 392). Clearly this perspective shares certain features
with the Walrasian general equilibrium perspective (in contrast
to the Marshallian emphasis on the single industry). But the
dynamic, competitive–entrepreneurial market process insights

that inform the Misesian perspective clearly mark that perspective as a Mengerian (and quintessentially Austrian), rather than Walrasian, point of view.

The Market Prices That Prevail
at a Given Moment

This chapter has emphasized Mises' view of the market process as one which, through steps of entrepreneurial discovery, tends to correct "maladjustments" (brought about by earlier entrepreneurial failure correctly to anticipate changing developments). In this view of things the market prices at any given instant are "*false* prices" (HA, 338; italics in original). It is because of their falsity that they are necessarily disequilibrium prices. It is the market through which profit-seeking entrepreneurs systematically tend to modify these prices, tending to ensure that they be replaced by prices which more closely and "truthfully" reflect the underlying preferences of consumers. But, while this is indeed the central theme in Mises' theory of the market process, there is also another, at first glance almost antithetical, theme in Mises' theory. This theme is the sense in which the real world market prices at any given moment are seen by Mises as the right prices, the "equilibrium" prices, the "market-clearing" prices. Government interference in these prices necessarily *worsens* matters.[12] We offer here a brief explanation of this second Misesian theme, in order both to show its consistency with the first theme we have been emphasizing and to show its importance in Mises' overall understanding of the market economy.

When Mises described the real-world market prices at any given instant as reflecting an "equilibrium of demand and supply" (HA, 762), he did not mean the demand-supply equilibrium of the mainstream neoclassical textbooks. The latter equilibrium state is one in which *all* participants (and all potential participants) in a specific market *have become aware of that price* which is capable of clearing the market, and *have correctly anticipated* that this market-clearing price would indeed prevail in the market. Equilibrium presumes complete and accurate mutual anticipation by each market participant of the actions of all other participants. There are *no* relevant "maladjustments" in the neoclassical equilibrium state. Obviously, Mises did *not* refer to the real-world prices at any given moment in any such omniscient context. Rather Mises was referring to what he called the "plain state of rest." In the Misesian plain state of rest all possible transactions *between those who have become aware of the possibility of such mutually beneficial transactions* have been completed. In Mises' scheme, this plain state of rest "comes to pass" in the real world "again and again." "At any instant all those transactions take place which the parties are ready to enter into at the realizable prices" (HA, 244). Clearly, these prices are "equilibrium" prices only in the very narrow sense that, *given current knowledge* on the part of market participants, these prices have permitted all known possibilities for exchange transactions to be realized. In no way are these prices—"false" as we have seen Mises to believe them to be—equilibrium prices in the sense of accurately expressing all conceivable mutually beneficial exchanges between market participants.

The reason why Mises nonetheless attached great significance to the spontaneous market prices at any instant, despite their "falsity," is quite straightforward. It has to do with the idea of *consumer sovereignty,* an idea which we have seen Mises to emphasize as central in understanding markets. For Mises the market prices at any given instant are, despite their falsity, the prices *completely* dictated by the sovereignty of the consumer— in the following somewhat special sense. These prices express the bids and offers of all market participants, and as such reflect the entrepreneurial judgment, as of that moment, of the brightest and most alert individuals, *in the light of what they believe will most effectively cater to the preferences of the consumer.* It is of course true that many of these bids and offers will have been made mistakenly, that is, will have been based on erroneous entrepreneurial judgment. But even these mistakes have been made under the pressure of consumer sovereignty. After all, "sovereignty" does not necessarily imply that all actions taken are "correct," in the sense of fulfilling the sovereign's will; it merely implies that all actions taken are taken with utmost seriousness and deliberation, *in order* to fulfil the sovereign's will. In this sense Mises saw the free market as *continuously* expressive of consumer sovereignty. From this perspective, well-meaning government interventions offering obstacles to the free movement of market prices constitute, *even where they are undertaken in order to correct alleged market failures of one kind or another,* an interference with the constant tendency of the free market to respect the sovereignty of consumers.

Mises and the Market Process

As we shall see in subsequent chapters, these ideas of Mises concerning the dynamically competitive–entrepreneurial market process, and concerning its consequent fulfillment of the notion of consumer sovereignty, were fundamental to his economics. In some respects (as in the simple analysis of government price-fixing), this perspective led Mises in paths hardly different from those pursued by mainstream neoclassical economists. In others (as in the assessment of "antitrust" policies believed to enhance the competitiveness of the market), Mises' perspective led him sharply to disagree with the mainstream. In all his economics, however, Mises consistently adhered to his own Mengerian and Austrian understanding of how the market works.

CHAPTER FIVE

MONETARY THEORY, CYCLE THEORY, AND THE RATE OF INTEREST

MISES' FIRST BOOK was *The Theory of Money and Credit* (1912). In addressing the field of monetary theory in that work, Mises applied the principles of the Austrian School as developed particularly by Menger and by Böhm-Bawerk—but in ways which went beyond the positions taken by his teachers. In Mises' own words: "The systems of Menger and Böhm-Bawerk were no longer wholly satisfactory to me. I was ready to proceed further on the road these old masters had discovered. But I could not use their treatment of those problems with which the monetary theorist must begin" (NR, 56). Mises' 1912 book followed some six years of study by Mises of monetary, currency, and banking issues, and had been preceded by several journal articles dealing with these topics. These topics were to take up a good deal of Mises' professional attention in the coming decades, and to result in several shorter, German-language works published in the twenties.[1] Mises returned, finally, to these same theoretical and applied issues in his 1949 *Human Action* (following on a similar treatment in his 1940 *Nationalökonomie.*)

In this chapter, we will attempt to outline Mises' contributions to monetary theory. We will also examine Mises' important role in developing what came to be known as the Austrian Theory of the Trade Cycle. (Mises' work in this regard was in fact first put forward in the concluding chapters of his 1912 book on monetary theory, as an aspect of the advanced theory of money.) We will conclude with a brief survey of Mises' views on the nature of capital and interest (topics which, in Mises' overall system of economics, had at least tangential relevance to his views on the theory of the trade cycle).

A. MONETARY THEORY

At the time of his 1912 book, much of Mises' monetary theory must have seemed novel, if not revolutionary. And if, as we shall see, his ideas required him to reject certain positions taken by his Austrian mentors, they constituted even more radical departures from the doctrines that were then dominant in the German monetary literature. In Mises' own retrospective account of the strongly negative reception accorded to his book in Germany, one can sense the defiant pride that Mises took in having decisively undermined the monetary doctrines generally accepted at the time of his youthful effort. "Men such as Knapp,

Bendixen, Liefmann, Diehl, Adolf Wagner and Bortkiewicz," Mises wrote in 1940, "who then were celebrated in Germany as 'monetary theorists' are no longer considered authorities." Clearly it was Mises' book which contributed significantly to the change in professional opinions. So successful was the book in this regard, indeed, that certain key elements in Mises' approach no longer appear today as fresh and as original as they must have appeared in 1912 and in the immediately following years. A fair treatment of Mises' contributions to economics must not, however, ignore the degree to which they pioneered in changing the climate of professional opinion—even to the point where they may seem, to today's readers, to be comfortably familiar.

The Radical Character of Mises' Approach

Mises has given us his own retrospective (1940) assessment of the radical purpose of his 1912 book. "According to prevailing opinion at that time, the theory of money could be clearly separated from the total structure of economic problems...; in a certain respect it was an independent discipline.... It was my intention to reveal this position as erroneous and restore the theory of money to its appropriate position as an integral part of the science of economics" (NR, 56).

To achieve this objective, Mises found it necessary to attack several strands of the conventional monetary-theoretic wisdom of his time. These included: (a) the dominant view that the

Austrian theory of marginal utility was inapplicable to the theory of the value of money; (b) the dominant view that money can be treated as "neutral" (i.e., that changes in the supply of money lead to changes in the purchasing power of money, but do not generate significant substantive changes in the ("real") structure of an economy; (c) the view (dominant in the German literature) that the state (i.e., the government) fills a role, in regard to the economic functions of money, categorically different from its role in regard to commercial transactions generally.

While each of these strands of then-conventional wisdom relates to a separate and distinct aspect of monetary theory, Mises' strongly dissenting positions on all three derived from a single taproot: his conviction that monetary theory must be recognized "as an integral part of the science of economics."

The Value of Money

At the time that Mises wrote his book, the dominant theory believed to account for the purchasing power of money was the Quantity Theory. Originating in sixteenth-century empirical observations and the insights of Bodin and Davanzati, the theory had had its ups and downs in professional opinion. By the start of the twentieth century the theory was fairly widely upheld, but the term "Quantity Theory of Money" had become quite elastic, covering a number of rather different versions.[2] As we shall see, Mises recognized the kernel of truth in these various versions of the Quantity Theory (and indeed defended the theory against a number of the objections of its critics). But his own positive theory explaining the way in which the purchasing power (the "value") of money is determined must be understood against the background of the Fisherine version of the Quantity Theory, a version which he vigorously attacked for what he considered its "mechanical" character (TMC, 144).[3] Mises was referring especially to Irving Fisher's 1911 book (with H. G. Brown), *The Purchasing Power of Money.* (Schumpeter remarked that ever since the publication of that book "Fisher has been classed as a sponsor of a particularly rigid form of quantity theory.")[4] The nub of this "mechanical," "rigid" version of the theory was, in Mises' words, its "conclusion that variations in the ratio between the quantity of money and the demand for it lead to proportionate variations in the objective exchange-value of money" (TMC, 144). Mises devoted considerable space to refuting this conclusion; he found it difficult to understand how economists familiar with the subjective theory of value could have fallen into the error it represented. The only explanation he could put forward had to do with their failure to integrate monetary theory with economic theory generally (a failure the correction of which was, as we have noted, a principle objective of Mises' book). "One thing only can explain how Fisher is able to maintain his mechanical Quantity Theory.

To him the Quantity Theory seems a doctrine peculiar to the value of money; in fact, he contrasts it outright with the laws of value of other economic goods" (TMC, 144).

The challenge which Mises set for himself was in fact to show that the theoretical explanation for the value of money is, in principle, exactly the *same* explanation (i.e., the subjective theory of value) that economists (at least since the marginal utility revolution of the early 1870s) used to account for *all* commodity market values. Mises recognized that he faced a formidable challenge. Until the appearance of his own work, he observed, "the subjective school" (by which he meant in particular the Austrians) had not succeeded in "developing a complete theory of the value of money on the basis of the subjective theory of value and its peculiar doctrine of marginal utility" (TMC, 114).

Perhaps the best known argument which had hitherto been advanced in order to claim that the standard marginal utility theory of value could *not* be used to account for the value of money was the "circularity" argument. Mises cited Helfferich (author of a well-known, German-language 1903 monetary treatise) on this point. Helfferich noted that marginal utility theory explains the exchange-value (i.e., the market prices) of goods by reference to the degree of utility that potential consumers attach to these goods. A similar explanation for the exchange-value (i.e., the purchasing power) of a unit of money would then have to proceed by reference to the degree of utility that potential users of money attach to that unit. But the utility attached to a unit of money is nothing else but "the amount of consumable goods that can be obtained in exchange for it.... The marginal utility of money...*presupposes* a certain exchange-value of the money; so the latter cannot be derived from the former" (TMC, 119-20; emphasis supplied). The marginal utility of a loaf of bread is independent of the price of bread. The marginal utility of a dollar is meaningful only in terms of the purchasing power of the dollar. To explain the purchasing power of the dollar by reference to its marginal utility is to fall into a circularity trap.

Now this circularity argument has been totally dismissed by some modern writers (notably by Don Patinkin, an eminent midcentury monetary theorist).[5] Mises, however, took the argument seriously and developed what came to be a well-known solution to the circularity problem. For purposes of present discussion it is not really important to explain what Patinkin's reasoning for his dismissal was, and why Mises would not have accepted that reasoning. (This is all the more so since this would involve us in "Austrian" considerations basically unrelated to Mises' contributions to monetary theory.)[6] For us, it is sufficient to note that, at the time Mises wrote his book, the circularity argument was treated with great respect. Mises, in advancing his own solution (his "regression theorem") for this problem, was addressing an important issue in the monetary-theoretic debates of his time. For Mises, perhaps the even more important implication of his regression theorem was his ability, with the use of this theorem, to integrate the theory of the value of money into the main body of value theory as developed by the subjective economics of the Austrian School.

Mises' Regression Theorem

Mises' solution to the circularity problem proceeded by distinguishing sharply between (a) the purchasing power of money as it enters into the marginal utility considerations of prospective demanders of money, and (b) the purchasing power of money (emerging out of the marginal-utility-driven choices of such prospective demanders) that we are seeking to explain. The circularity problem exists only if one fails to recognize this distinction (so that a marginal utility explanation of the purchasing power of money would *appear* to involve a circularity). "The difficulty is, however, merely apparent. The purchasing power which we explain...is not the same purchasing power the height of which determines...demand. The problem is...the determination of the purchasing power of the immediate future.... For the solution of this problem we refer to the purchasing power of the immediate past.... These are two distinct magnitudes. It is erroneous to object to our theorem...that it moves in a vicious circle" (HA, 408 f).

The purchasing power that informs the decisions of potential individual demanders of money is the purchasing power that they *expect* to reside in units of money that they may acquire. Mises postulated that this *expected* purchasing power will generally be assumed to be what it has in fact been in the immediate *past*. As a result of the interaction between innumerable individual market participants, each basing his marginal utility calculations on the *past* purchasing power of money, the market generates—at each moment—a new market value for money—that is, a new purchasing power of money, which may well be (but of course need not be) at a different level than that of the past purchasing power which informed the individual calculations.

Mises recognized, of course, that this seems to push us back into an endless historical regression. Each day's purchasing power of money is determined, it would seem, by that of the preceding day. This would seem to be an endless sequence of "explanations," and thus a sequence unable to provide us with an independent starting point to serve as an explanatory element. But Mises maintained that this historical regression was not endless. Building on Menger's theory of how the institution of money can be understood to have emerged spontaneously out of prehistoric barter markets (TMC, 30-34), Mises points out that the historical regression which he has outlined for us need (and can) proceed back only to the moment when the monetary commodity first came to be valued, to some extent at least, as a common medium of exchange. Up until that point in time the market value of this commodity was determined entirely by marginal utility considerations that did *not* include (and were thus entirely independent of) purchasing power considerations. "At this point yesterday's exchange value is exclusively determined by the non-monetary...demand which is displayed only by those who want to use this good for other employments than that of a medium of exchange" (HA, 409).

Mises had thus succeeded in using the Austrian School's marginal utility theory of value to explain the determination of the value of money. And it is here that Mises found a place for what he considered the kernel of truth in the Quantity Theory of the value of money. "[T]he idea that a connexion exists between the variations in the value of money on the one hand and variations in the relations between the demand for money and the supply of it on the other hand,...constitutes the core of truth in the [Quantity] theory..." (TMC, 130). His main objections to the more mechanical versions of the Quantity Theory were closely related to his objections to widespread views concerning the desirability and possibility of "neutral" money.

The Concept of Neutral Money

The term "neutral money" was not in general professional use when Mises wrote his 1912 book, and he did not couch his criticisms of the Quantity Theory explicitly in terms of this idea. (Hayek attributes the term itself to Wicksell, who used it "more or less incidentally, and without the intention to introduce it as a technical term.")[7] Friedrich Lutz credits Hayek's writings of the early thirties as being "largely responsible for its adoption...as a technical term by economists in the English-speaking world."[8] There is no doubt, however, that Mises' criticisms in 1912 (which are fundamentally identical with those with which, in his 1949 *Human Action,* he *did* explicitly attack the neutral money idea) were directed at the *idea,* if not the term, of neutral money. The idea of neutral money was closely bound up with the view of the theory of money as conceivable separately from the theory of the market economy in general.[9] It was the idea that, in a general equilibrium system, exchange can be conceived of as occurring through the medium of a *numeraire,* a system in which there are no cash holdings. The "'money' of this system is not a medium of exchange; it is not money at all; it is merely a *numeraire,* an ethereal and undetermined unit of accounting of that vague and indefinable character which the fancy of some economists...have attributed to money" (HA, 249). This view of money's neutrality held that the theory of exchange "can be elaborated under the assumption that there is direct exchange [i.e., barter] only.... It was not believed that [the introduction of money into the theory] could alter anything essential in the structure of economic teachings. The main task of economics was conceived as the study of direct exchange" (HA, 202).

We have already noted Mises' criticism of Fisher (and Brown) for believing that "variations in the ratio between the quantity of money and the demand for it lead to proportionate variations in the objective exchange-value of money." Mises' objections rested on his insight that money, like all economic goods in the real world, enters into the realm of market exchange as a *dynamic factor*. As early as 1912 he wrote: "All those who ascribe to variations in the quantity of money an inverse proportionate effect on the value of the monetary unit are applying to dynamic conditions a method of analysis that is only suitable for static condition." (TMC, 145). Three and a half decades later he expressed his critique of the idea of neutral money in similar terms: "Money is necessarily a 'dynamic factor'; there is no room left for money in a 'static' system" (HA, 249). It is the "spurious idea of the supposed neutrality of money" that is responsible for the "notion of the 'level' of prices that rises or falls proportionately with the increase or decrease in the quantity of money in circulation. It was not realized that changes in the quantity of money can never affect the prices of all goods and services at the same time and to the same extent" (HA, 398 f).

Not only did Mises criticize the idea of any money in fact being neutral. He also attacked the idea that there is something desirable in the supposed neutrality of money. The idea of neutral money (changes in the quantity of which can be supposed not to affect the structure of prices and quantities in the "real" sector) is a chimera. "Money, without a driving force of its own would not, as people assume, be a perfect money; it would not be money at all" (HA, 418). There is nothing perfect about a supposedly neutral money. In a world of action and change, neutrality is simply impossible. "It is therefore neither strange nor vicious that in a frame of...a changing world money is neither neutral nor stable in purchasing power.... Money is an element of action and consequently of change" (HA, 419). In this critique of the neutral money idea, Mises is consistently applying the dynamic-theoretic perspective for the understanding of market processes, which we outlined in chapter 4, to the monetary aspects of those processes. His monetary theory categorically refuses to recognize any gulf separating the theory of money from the economic theory of markets in general. The circumstance that the market process consists of series of exchanges, virtually all of which involve a commonly used medium of exchange, makes it crucially important to recognize how its use vitally and actively affects the pattern and structure of production and exchange decisions made. The integration of monetary theory into general economic theory grows out of our understanding that the idea of neutral money is empirically irrelevant and analytically obfuscating. All this is closely related to Mises' rejection of one of the most popular elements in the monetary theory of his time, the so-called State Theory of Money.

The State Theory of Money

One of the most influential books on money during the years when Mises was writing his own *Theorie des Geldes und der Umlaufsmittel* was a work by an eminent German economist of the Historical School, Georg Friedrich Knapp. *Die Staatliche Theorie des Geldes* appeared in 1905 and enjoyed remarkable success.[10] Although certainly not the first to advance such a theory, "Knapp's exposition was extremely effective. His forceful dogmatism and his original conceptualization of his theory impressed laymen and those economists who were laymen in economic theory."[11] His thesis was a simple one: "Money is the Creature of Law."[12] The institution of money was essentially an invention of the state; and it is the state which determines which commodity is to serve as money. Now Menger had already, in effect, rejected Knapp's theory. Both in his 1871 *Grundsätze* and in an 1892 encyclopedia article titled "Geld"[13] (and also elsewhere), Menger had developed the theme that money "is one of the spontaneous, unconscious, unplanned social discoveries, which are not inventions of the State or products of a legislative act, as Knapp was to emphasize."[14] (In fact Mises reports that, when he used to raise Knapp's work in conversation with Menger, the latter used to refer to it in most contemptuous terms, and to express derisive dismay at its popularity in Germany [NR, 35].)[15] One implication of Knapp's theory had rather obvious political resonance. As Schumpeter put it: "[M]any people and especially politicians at that time welcomed a theory that seemed to offer a basis for the growing popularity of state-managed money." Moreover, as Schumpeter noted, "during the First World War [Knapp's theory] was in fact widely used to 'prove' that the inflation of the currency had nothing to do with soaring prices."[16] In Mises' terminology, Knapp's theory of money was an "acatallactic" theory, one that "cannot be built into any system that deals realistically with the processes of economic activity." It is, Mises asserted, "utterly impossible to employ [acatallactic theories] as foundations for a theory of exchange" (TMC, 461).[17]

In refuting Knapp's theory, therefore, Mises was not merely reaffirming Menger's rejection of this *genre* of monetary theories, he was rejecting the idea that monetary phenomena can be separated analytically from the general phenomena of market exchanges. We have seen in chapter 3 that Mises emphasized the insight, provided by the development of a science of economics, that there are regularities ("laws") in economic phenomena to which governments must pay heed, and to which they must adjust their policies. The rejection of economics by politicians and others seeking to declare the absolute power of the government in achieving its economic objectives for society, we saw, had much to do with the realization that economics teaches the inevitable limits to such power. Mises' rejection of the State Theory of Money was a consistent extension of this Misesian perspective on the tension between economic science and absolute political power. The dichotomy (conceded, in effect, even by economists of the Austrian School up to that time) between the monetary sector (and monetary theory) and the real exchange economy (and general economic theory)—a dichotomy against which Mises was battling in his 1912 work—was virtually an acknowledgment of the absolute power of the state in the monetary area. Mises was explicit in refusing to recognize this or any other such exception.

"The position of the State in the market," he wrote, "differs in no way from that of any other parties to commercial transactions.... If it wishes to alter any of the exchange-ratios established in the market, it can only do this through the market's own mechanism.... [It] cannot set aside the laws of the pricing process" (TMC, 68). Mises cited famous examples of the inevitable "failure of authoritative interference with the market" (TMC, 68). He proceeded immediately to the consistent conclusion: "The concept of money as a creature of Law and the State is clearly untenable.... To ascribe to the State the power of dictating the laws of exchange, is to ignore the fundamental principle of money-using society" (TMC, 69). In other words, just as governments must adjust to the laws of the market (so that they must be aware that attempts to fix prices will have inevitable—and unwelcome—consequences), so too must governments be aware that the laws of the market apply to monetary phenomena as well (so that, for example, they realize that attempts to achieve their own economic objectives for society by printing more money will have inevitable, market-generated consequences that, indeed, can be disastrously unwelcome).

B. TRADE CYCLE THEORY

We have noted Mises' decisive rejection of the notion of "neutral money." One direct manifestation of this rejection was Mises' pioneering work in what came to be known as the Austrian (or, sometimes, the Mises-Hayek) Theory of the Trade Cycle. Mises' contribution was first advanced, in no more than several pages, in the closing chapters of his 1912 work on monetary theory. Consistent development of his foundational ideas on money as an integral element in the exchange economy led Mises to offer an outline of the way in which changes in the supply of money can lead (in fact, in Mises' view, must *inevitably* lead) to structural aberrations in the pattern of production and exchanges, the inevitable corrections to which by the market must express themselves as what we know as the crisis and depression phases of the trade cycle. Mises developed these ideas further in his 1928 monograph (translated under the title *Monetary Stabilization and Cyclical Policy*) and in his later treatises (*Nationalökonomie*, 1940, and *Human Action*, 1949).

It must be acknowledged that certain ambiguities surround the relation between Mises' contribution to the theory of the trade cycle, and antecedent ideas which Mises cited from both the British Currency School, developed before the middle of the nineteenth century, and the great Swedish economist Knut Wicksell around the turn of the century. Ambiguities also surround the relation between Mises' contribution to the more fully articulated (and much better known) theory of Hayek which the latter developed in the early 1930s. Sometimes Mises himself seemed to downplay his own role in the "Austrian" theory,[18] even questioning the appropriateness of the "Austrian" label in the light of the antecedent British and Swedish ideas. But, in his 1940 memoirs, in referring to the theory of business cycle phenomena, he wrote: "I am honored that it was named the Austrian Trade Cycle Theory" (NR, 61).

Hayek's first (1925) published reference to the "Austrian" theory of the cycle cites only one source, Mises' 1924 edition of his 1912 book. (In his 1984 introduction to the publication of English translations of a number of his papers of the 1920s, Hayek singles out that first published reference of his and refers to "what I thought was a theory of Ludwig von Mises that was familiar to us in the Vienna circle.")[19] In his *Monetary Theory and the Trade Cycle* (1933; a translation and revision of the German *Geldtheorie und Konjunkturtheorie* published in 1929), Hayek cites Mises extensively. Yet the preface to the first edition (1931) of his

Prices and Production did not, surprisingly, mention Mises among his acknowledgments to intellectual predecessors. Hayek seemed, in his preface to the second (1934) edition of the same work, to go out of his way to add Mises to his list of intellectual predecessors. Apparently, Hayek (at least in the first edition), while certainly recognizing Mises' role in suggesting the *monetary* aspect of the Austrian Cycle Theory, saw his own work on the "real" aspects of the cycle as stemming more generally from Austrian capital theory.[20]

There seems little doubt, however, that the core of the "Austrian" (or even the "Hayekian") Theory of the Trade Cycle ultimately derives, virtually entirely, from the pioneering work contained in those few pages in Mises' 1912 treatise on monetary theory. Certainly, the theory outlined in those pages owed much to the earlier ideas acknowledged by Mises; and it is unquestionably the case that it was Hayek's careful and original elaboration in the 1930s of the Misesian outline which became best known to the economics profession. Despite all this, however, no account of Mises' contributions can fail to recognize the pivotal role played by Mises' own theory of the trade cycle. Writing in 1951, Ludwig Lachmann put it this way: "Almost forty years ago Professor Mises, through a brilliant interpretation of an idea of Wicksell, became the first exponent of what has come to be known as 'The Austrian Theory of the Trade Cycle.'"[21]

The Misesian Theory of the Trade Cycle

Mises apparently did not, in 1912, *set out* to provide a theory of
the trade cycle. His theory emerged as an almost incidental by-
product of his exploration of the theory of banking (especially
the influence of the banking system which results from its ability to issue "fiduciary media"). The term "fiduciary media" was
apparently introduced by H. E. Batson, the 1934 translator of
the second edition of Mises' book into English (TMC, appendix
B, 482), but Mises himself adopted this term for his own use in
his later work. Mises defined "fiduciary media" as that amount
of "money-substitutes"[22] against which the debtors do *not* in
fact keep a 100 percent reserve of "money proper " (HA, 433).

In the course of this exploration, Mises examined the influence on the rate of interest exercised by an expansion in the
issue of fiduciary media. Following Wicksell, Mises concluded
that such expansion would reduce the "money rate of interest"
("the rate of interest that is demanded and paid for loans in
money or money-substitutes") below the "natural rate of interest" (the rate "that would be determined by supply and demand if actual capital goods were lent without the mediation of
money") (TMC, 355). He then examined the consequences of the
resulting "Wicksellian" divergence of the money rate of interest
below the natural rate. Using Böhm-Bawerkian capital-and-in-
terest theory (TMC, 339 n), he demonstrated that the conse-

quence would be a tendency for producers to enter into more "roundabout" processes of production than are in fact warranted by the true availability of consumer goods that will be needed "to support the labourers and entrepreneurs during the longer period" (TMC, 361). Mises then traced the series of market reactions through which the "equilibrium of the loan market is re-established after it has been disturbed by the intervention of the banks" (TMC, 362). Because the "period of production" has been lengthened more than is consistent with the underlying facts, an inevitable consequence must be the "reduction of the quantity of goods available for consumption. The market prices of consumption goods rise and those of production goods fall.... That is, the rate of interest on loans rises again, it again approaches the natural rate" (TMC, 362-3). (Mises is *extremely* brief in this last statement. He relies on the reader's understanding of the Böhm-Bawerkian insight that the money rate of interest simply corresponds, in a smoothly running economy at a given level of production, to the excess value of consumer goods at a given date, over the value—the spot prices—of the inputs invested at an earlier date in their production.)

This understanding of how the money rate of interest, initially depressed by bank fiduciary media expansion, is forced back up by reassertion in the market of the underlying realities (i.e., the refusal by consumers to postpone their demand for immediate consumption goods), leads directly to a theory of crises. Mises sees the economic crisis as expressing "the loss of some of the capital invested in the excessively-lengthened round-about processes of production. It is not practicable to transfer all of the production goods from those uses that have proved unprofitable [because the market has pushed interest rates higher than the levels that had previously made those longer processes appear to be profitable] into other avenues of employment...there is a loss of value.... Economic goods which could have satisfied more important wants have been employed for the satisfaction of less important" (TMC, 364). Insofar as many of these capital inputs are specific and not easily transferable, entrepreneurs suffer losses, and are forced to cancel projects. As Mises asserts: "Our theory of banking...leads ultimately to a theory of business cycles" (TMC, 365).

Mises maintained this theory of the business cycle, apart from minor revisions, both in his 1928 monograph and in his 1949 treatise. And although Hayek developed the "real" elements of the business cycle theory far more carefully and extensively in his 1931 *Prices and Production*, it does seem fair to bracket Mises and Hayek as having adhered basically to the same, shared, theory.[23] In his classic League of Nations volume surveying and classifying theories of the business cycle, Gottfried Haberler lists, in alphabetical order, Hayek, Machlup, Mises, Robbins, Röpke, and Strigl as exponents of what he called the neo-Wicksellian version of the "monetary over-investment theory" of the business cycle.[24] Clearly, Mises was the source for almost of all these writers, most of whom—as well as Haberler himself—were Mises' disciples in one sense or another. Haberler recognizes that while Wicksell "has provided the theoretical basis for this theory," Wicksell himself followed a different theory of the business cycle.

Certain characteristic features of the Misesian theory should be emphasized:

(a) The theory finds the source of the cycle problem to lie in the expansion of the money supply. (Mises' theory of banking demonstrates the ability of the banking system to achieve such expansion.) In this, Mises saw himself as a follower of those British economists of the mid-nineteenth century who offered the Currency School's explanation, in terms of monetary expansion, for the crises of its time.

(b) Mises' theory then follows Wicksell in focusing attention upon the way in which such monetary expansion generates a money rate of interest that is systematically (and misleadingly) below that natural rate of interest which expresses the true willingness of market participants to postpone immediate consumption enjoyments for the sake of greater future gains.

(c) The theory then traces the consequences of this aberration for the production plans undertaken by entrepreneurs. They are led to make irreversible, but "erroneous," plans based on the *apparent* profitability of such plans (as reflecting the falsely low rates of money interest). These errors will inevitably be revealed;

their revelation manifests itself in the form of abandoned projects and sudden drastic reductions in the market values of those projects.

(d) The erroneous quality of these production plans consists in their requiring consumers (because of the longer "waiting period" entailed by greater "roundaboutness") to be denied a greater volume of immediate consumer goods than these consumers are in fact prepared to agree to. It is here that the Austrian focus on the time-dimension of production finds its expression. It is the rate of interest which has the function of balancing the desire of consumers for consumption goods *now* with their desire for a compensatingly larger volume of such consumption goods *later*. The misleadingly low money rate of interest encourages producers to ignore the true needs of consumers for immediate consumer satisfactions. But these ignored underlying truths will inevitably emerge—in the form of shortages of consumer goods which push up their prices to the point where the rate of interest has been forced by the market toward its "true," natural level. This latter correction, revealing the errors of production processes begun under false assumptions, takes the form, as we have seen, of the crisis phase of the business cycle. In *Human Action,* Mises put it this way: "The whole entrepreneurial class is, as it were [during the boom phase of the cycle], in the position of a master-builder whose task it is to erect a building out of a limited supply of building materials. If this man overestimates the quantity of the available supply, he drafts a plan for the execution of which the means at his disposal are not sufficient. He oversizes the groundwork and the foundations and only discovers later in the progress of the construction that he lacks the material needed for the completion of the structure" (TMC, 560). The loss of value, the abandonment of projects in midstream, which occur during the crisis and downturn phases of the cycle, are clearly analogous to the unfinished, abandoned buildings.

(e) The entire thrust of the theory is that it serves as a textbook example of the *non*-neutrality of money. Monetary expansion certainly has affected—in disastrous fashion—the structure of the real production economy.

In his 1912 outline of the theory, Mises does not appear to have explicitly attributed to the government any crucial role in the monetary expansion responsible for the boom phase of the cycle (and thus, in Mises' theory, for the eventual crisis phase and subsequent depression). But in his 1928 and 1949 treatments, Mises is most emphatic in laying at the door of governmentally installed central banks the ultimate responsibility for the distortions (and eventually the depressions) which arise out of the expansion of fiduciary media. He refers, in particular, to the practice of considering it the duty of central banks of issue "to shield the banks which expanded circulation credit from the consequences of their conduct," in order to soften the economic hardships experienced during the crisis.[25] Mises was caustic in his condemnation of such public policy attitudes. The "practice of intervening for the benefit of banks, rendered insolvent by the crisis, and of the customers of these banks, has resulted in suspending the market forces which could serve to prevent a return of the expansion. If the banks emerge from the crisis unscathed...what remains to restrain them from embarking once more on an attempt to reduce artificially the interest rate on loans and expand circulation credit...?"[26]

In *Human Action,* Mises developed the thesis that, in the absence of central bank control over the banking system, competition between private banks in the market would tend to limit credit expansion (and thus remove the source of the business cycle aberrations). "Government interference" in the banking sector is therefore held ultimately responsible for credit expansion. This policy of encouraging credit expansion has its source in "the erroneous assumption that credit expansion is a proper means of lowering the rate of interest permanently and without harm to anybody but the callous capitalists" (HA, 443 f). Quoting from Mises' 1928 discussion, Haberler cites Mises as maintaining that the root cause of the cyclical character (of the boom and its aftermath) is the ideology which considers the reduction of the rate of interest to be desirable and the inflationary expansion of credit to be the best way of achieving that objective."[27]

But this ideology in favor of lower interest rates is based, Mises believed, in economic ignorance. Market-generated rates of interest have an important economic function to perform and arise out of an essential aspect of human nature. And it is to Mises' radically "Austrian" theory of capital and interest to which we now turn.[28]

C. THE THEORY OF CAPITAL
AND INTEREST

As we have seen, the "Austrian" Theory of the Trade Cycle combined a key Wicksellian insight (on the divergence between the "money" rate of interest and the "natural" rate of interest) with ideas concerning the time-dimension of production, which had their source in Böhm-Bawerk's famous theories concerning capital and interest. Mises accepted key elements from Böhm-Bawerk's theories; but he also gradually grew dissatisfied with other elements in those theories. The first edition of his 1912 *Theorie des Geldes und der Umlaufsmittel* used Böhm-Bawerk's approach to the theory of capital-using production and interest without reservations. His 1924 second edition of that work, however, contained a rather lengthy footnote both praising Böhm-Bawerk for a "great achievement" and indicating some serious disagreement with his approach (TMC, 339n). Mises also used that footnote to refer to an anticipated "special study" of his own on the problem of interest, which he hoped would "appear in the not-too-distant future." That special study never did appear, and apart from a number of brief observations on the area of capital and interest which appeared in various writings of

Mises over the years, it was not until his 1940 treatise, *Nationalökonomie,* that Mises presented his complete theory of interest (along with a series of carefully formulated statements concerning the use of the term "capital" in theoretical discussion, with special critical emphasis upon its use in discussions of interest theory). This theory of interest he developed was so radical and so striking that when Frank Knight wrote his 1941 review article, he chose to concentrate virtually his entire discussion—in an article highly critical of Mises—on that topic, entitling it "Professor Mises and the Theory of Capital."[29]

There are certain fascinating highlights in the history of theories of capital and interest that are reflected in Knight's trenchant article. Knight was himself, it should be noted, the author of an approach to capital and interest theory which was advanced as a vigorously argued alternative to the Böhm-Bawerkian (i.e., the "Austrian") theory. (In fact Knight was endorsing and expanding on positions taken much earlier by the U.S. economist John Bates Clark, who had engaged in a celebrated controversy with Böhm-Bawerk around the turn of the century.) Knight had objected to key "Austrian" features of Böhm-Bawerk's theories; his criticisms of Mises' 1940 treatment of these issues arose out of the circumstance that Mises was even more "Austrian" than his mentor (Böhm-Bawerk) had been. What aroused Knight's analytical ire in Mises was, in particular, those areas in which Mises believed that his mentor had not proceeded consistently enough, or far enough, in the strictly "Austrian" (i.e., subjective) direction.

This is not the place for a detailed account of the agreements and disagreements between Böhm-Bawerk, Mises, and Knight.[30] But it is important to indicate some of the doctrinal background against which we must try to understand Mises' own positions on, and his contributions to, the theory of capital and interest. These positions reflect profound philosophical insights that Mises translated into the logic of their economic implications. Yet much in Mises' position has left many of his readers—even those not nearly as critical of Mises as Knight was—puzzled. In the following we attempt to outline Mises' position as clearly as possible, while recognizing some of the difficulties that many of his readers have encountered.

Capital, Interest, and Time

Mises built solidly on the Böhm-Bawerkian insights concerning time; where he differed with Böhm-Bawerk was in his insistence on a more radically subjective perspective on the role of time than he found in his mentor's work. Mises emphasized his debt to "the imperishable merits of Böhm-Bawerk's contributions," in regard to the role of time (HA, 489); but he was not satisfied with his teacher's treatment. Böhm-Bawerk had emphasized the fact that production is a time-consuming ("roundabout") process; he had used this time-dimension of production as the source of explanation for the phenomenon of interest in a producing economy. For Böhm-Bawerk, interest emerged because entrepreneur-producers must, in order to engage today in time-consuming processes of production, persuade owners of resources to advance the services of their resources in processes, the fruits of which can be expected only at a later date. Resource owners will not, Böhm-Bawerk believed, be prepared to do so (i.e., to forgo more immediate extraction of consumer satisfaction from these owned resources) unless the fruits of these time-consuming production processes exceed in value alternative rewards available to these resource owners through immediate exchanges in today's spot markets. They will not be prepared to do so because of what came to be called "positive time preference"—a term loosely referring to preference for immediate, rather than postponed, reward. Mises took issue with the reliance which Böhm-Bawerk placed on the *psychological* basis for positive time preference (we shall refer briefly to this issue later on). In addition, he believed that Böhm-Bawerk had, surprisingly, become a victim of a fallacy which Böhm-Bawerk had himself prominently refuted: the belief that interest emerges as a result of the productivity of capital.

Earlier theorists had believed that since time-consuming processes of production require capital, it is the *productivity* of capital, manifested in the enhanced value of the fruits of time-consuming production processes, which is the source of interest.

Interest was seen as the fruit of a tree called "capital." Mises read Böhm-Bawerk's theory of interest as somehow still recognizing a role, in the generation of interest, played by the higher productivity of longer, more "roundabout" processes. Mises (following, in this regard, earlier work of the U.S. economist F. A. Fetter) found this to be inexplicable. Böhm-Bawerk had himself demonstrated the fallacy of the productivity theory of interest. If a tree is expected today to produce a steady annual stream of fruit in future years, this productivity will be entirely reflected in the tree's current market value. If a capital good can, through its investment today in a time-consuming process of production, generate a high-valued stream of output in the future, the value of that output will tend to be fully anticipated in today's market value of that capital good. This value will, in the absence of other causes for an interest phenomenon, rise to the point where the *physical* productivity of the capital good will be utterly unable to provide any flow of *value* return like the kind that we find in the real-world phenomenon of interest. Mises found it simply unintelligible that Böhm-Bawerk, who had so thoroughly and trenchantly deployed this kind of reasoning to refute the earlier productivity theorists, should have himself reverted to a theory which included productivity elements.

Mises found Böhm-Bawerk's treatment to be also faulty in the latter's discussions of time as if it somehow comes to be "congealed" in the durable things produced during time-con-

suming production processes. For Mises, time enters our understanding of the phenomena of interest strictly in its ex ante sense.
In making decisions in a multi-period world, producers, consumers, and resource owners treat time in a *forward-looking*
manner. An economics that focuses analytically (as Austrian
economics does) upon *decisions* rather than upon *things,* cannot,
therefore, treat time in its elapsed sense. It is this fact which led
Mises to reject an important element in the Böhm-Bawerkian
system: the elapsed, "average period of production." For Mises,
the role that time "plays in action consists entirely in the *choices*
acting man makes between periods of production of different
length. The length of time expended in the past for the production of capital goods available today does not count at all.... The
'average period of production' is an empty concept" (HA, 488-9;
emphasis supplied). Mises had apparently carefully studied the
ideas of philosophers regarding the nature of time, drawing
particularly on Henri Bergson. Mises identified the idea of time
as "a praxeological category." "Action is always directed toward
the future." "The present offers to acting opportunities and tasks
for which it was hitherto too early, and for which it will be
hereafter too late" (HA, 100-1). From this perspective, it is clear
that Mises could not endorse the Böhm-Bawerk-Hayek notion
that the capital stock of a society, at a given point in time,
possesses a "time-structure." (Hayek's use of this concept constitutes one significant difference between his own elaboration of

the Austrian Theory of the Trade Cycle and that of Mises.)

Indeed, Mises objected altogether to the use of the term "capital" to refer to the "totality of the produced factors of production." Such a totality is "a description of a part of the universe" that is "of no use in acting." Moreover, the use of a notion like aggregate "real capital" had been responsible for the "blunder" of explaining interest "as an income derived from the productivity of capital" (HA, 263). Instead, Mises endorsed Menger's use of the term capital as an accounting concept. "Capital is the sum of the money equivalent of all assets minus the sum of the money equivalent of all liabilities as dedicated at a definite date to the conduct of the operations of a definite business unit" (HA, 262). Capital is a correlate of the accounting notion of income. "The calculating mind of the actor draws a boundary line between the consumer's goods which he plans to employ for the immediate satisfaction of his wants and goods of all orders...which he plans to employ for providing by further acting, for the satisfaction of future wants.... That amount which can be consumed within a definite period without lowering the capital is called income." This use of the term "capital" is sharply distinguished, in Mises' terminology, from the term "capital goods." The presence of capital goods (produced factors of production) attests to the adoption by producers of time-consuming production processes. But there is no need whatsoever to refer to the totality of such capital goods. And "[t]here is no question of an alleged productivity of capital goods" (HA, 493); if it is profitable to engage in a time consuming process of production this is attributable entirely to the selection by the producer of the appropriate time-profile for the production process.

For Mises, then, the phenomenon of interest is in no sense a correlate of anything that might be called capital or capital goods. Although interest typically emerges in a world that uses capital goods, and in which capital accounting plays a crucially important role, interest is not the productivity return on any abstract totality that might be called "capital," nor is it the expression of the "productivity" of capital goods.

Instead, interest represents the economic manifestation of what Mises believed to be a universal (a "categorial") element in human action, the element of positive time preference. This element generates a characteristic pattern in the structure of inter-period prices, which expresses itself, in the loan market, as what we know as the phenomenon of interest. The element of time preference and the existence of the phenomenon of interest do not in any way *depend* on the role of production in economic life. "Productivity" is *not* the source of interest. Interest would occur even in a world in which no production takes place. But in our world, in which production *does* take place, the phenomenon of interest generates profoundly important implications. Because production takes time, the market decisions of producers, resource owners, and consumers, must very definitely take account of the interest phenomenon. The choice by producers of a process of production must pay careful attention to the length of time involved, for the duration of which interest will have to be paid. The choices made will of course determine (and be expressed in) the kind and durability of the tools (the "capital goods") that will be developed and deployed, the technology that will be utilized, and the kind and durability of the produced consumer goods. The inter-temporal market, the market in which producing entrepreneurs necessarily function, tends to ensure that prices (including the rates of interest) guide decision makers to take appropriate account of both the time preferences of market participants (resource owners and consumers) and the production possibilities associated with alternative production processes (involving different technologies and different time profiles).

It is this perspective upon the nature and market function of interest which undergirded Mises' lifelong concern with the dangers represented by ideologies and political programs that considered it possible and desirable to eliminate interest, or at least to engineer reduction in its rate. As we have seen in this chapter, it was this kind of ideological misunderstanding concerning interest that Mises blamed for the pain and suffering implicit in the trade cycle. Artificially low interest rates resulting from the expansion of the money supply (through "fiduciary media" creation) tends to distort production decisions, misleading producers to undertake processes of production unwarranted (in the length of their time profiles) by the inter-period structure of consumer preferences. As we saw earlier, a portion of the stock of capital goods assembled by producers will sooner or later suffer a severe loss of market value, as projects come necessarily to be abandoned as the true time preferences of market participants reassert themselves.

The Nature and the Source of Positive Time Preferences

Virtually everything presented in the preceding section as Mises' views (on interest and capital-using production) could rest on an understanding of positive time preference as a widely observed empirical phenomenon rooted in commonly encountered psychological regularities. But Mises was emphatic in insisting on the "categorial" character of the time preference phenomenon. One of the sources of Mises' dissatisfaction with Böhm-Bawerk's views on interest arises precisely out of this position. Böhm-Bawerk's "demonstration of the universal validity of time preference is inadequate," Mises maintained, "because it is based on psychological considerations" (HA, 488). For Mises, on the other hand, time preference emerges as a "praxeological theorem," flowing out of the essential quality of human action. "Time preference is a categorial requisite of human action. No mode of action can be thought of in which satisfaction within a nearer period of the future is not—other things being

equal—preferred to that of a later period. The very act of gratifying a desire implies that gratification at the present instant is
preferred to that at a later instant" (HA, 484).

Readers of Mises have had difficulty in appreciating this
characteristic example of Misesian a priorism. Mises himself
grappled with a number of the problems found with (and the
counter-examples offered against) this view of time preference as
embedded categorically in the very notion of action (HA, 489).
However, relatively few followers of Mises have found it necessary
to accept his views on this matter. It is perhaps worthwhile to
point out, nonetheless, that quite apart from the question of
whether positive time preference is simply an empirical regularity, or something which emerges inescapably from the very logic
of human action, Mises' notion of time preference is not quite the
same as that to be found in mainstream neoclassical treatments
of interest. These neoclassical treatments follow the path marked
out by the prominent early-twentieth-century American economist Irving Fisher (especially in his 1930 *The Theory of Interest*).

Fisher developed a neoclassical theory of interest which, following Böhm-Bawerk's "Austrian" approach to a considerable
extent, saw interest as resulting from the interplay between subjective elements (based on time preference, or, in Fisher's terminology, "impatience") and objective elements (the physical productivity of more time-consuming production processes). In
Fisher's theory (and in modern more technically sophisticated

versions of that theory) time preference expresses itself as a preference between *dates*—receipts available at date t_1 are preferred to receipts available at date t_2 (since t_2 is later than t_1).

Now it seems easy to imagine scenarios in which an individual *might* prefer the receipt of an item at the later (t_2) date rather than at the earlier (t_1) date. Someone in winter might prefer to receive a load of ice in six month's time (during the summer) rather than now. A prospective student might, in the year 2001, prefer to receive the academic calendar for the 2002-2003 academic year a year later (rather than immediately). These possibilities need not worry a neoclassical economist who builds his ideas of positive time preference on observed empirical regularities; these cases will be considered as relatively unusual cases that do not disturb the validity of the general assumption of positive time preference. But for Mises, who argues for the logical *inevitability* of positive time preference, such exceptions have sometimes been thought to pose problems.

However we should recognize that these kinds of "exceptions" do not qualify as cases of negative time preference *at all*. (This itself has nothing to do with the question of whether or not positive time preference is *logically* entailed by the very concept of human action.) For Mises, wherever the specific *date* (at which an item is to be received) alters its valuation in the eyes of an agent, *regardless of that date's closeness (to the moment at which preferences are registered)*, this means that it is the date itself (rather

than its *distance in time* from the moment of evaluation) that is
governing the evaluation. For Mises, time preference refers not
to dates, but to *future distance* from the moment of evaluation.
Of course the date *at* which ice is available, the date *at* which an
academic calendar is available, may affect its subjective evaluation. But for Mises, *that* kind of influence upon valuation is not
what he understood by the notion of time preference. Time
preference, for Mises, refers to the *sense of futurity.* A given receipt anticipated further in the future is valued (now), with
positive time preference, at a relatively lower level than that
same receipt anticipated sooner in the future. The notion of "a
given receipt" may certainly itself be affected by circumstances,
such as summer heat, which are associated with *date.* In Mises'
terminology, however, time preference is unaffected by such
considerations; Misesian time preference is relevant to *futurity,*
not to dates. One may not be prepared to follow Mises in seeing the logical inevitability of positive time preference. Nonetheless one should recognize that such "exceptions" as ice-next-
summer versus ice-in-today's-winter do not, for Mises, challenge any such claimed inevitability.

Money, Cycles, and Interest:
Concluding Observations

Many if not most of the policy debates between economists,
and between the exponents of clashing political positions on

economic affairs during the twentieth century have concerned the topics dealt with in this chapter. For the central decades of this century the dominant orthodoxy in the economics profession endorsed, in regard to these debates, the theoretical perspectives and policies associated with the work of John Maynard Keynes.[31] The Keynesian perspective focused attention on the interaction between key *aggregate* economic variables; it generated, in this way, an entirely new branch of economics, macroeconomics. This macroeconomic perspective focused attention, in particular, upon the adequacy of *aggregate demand* to sustain the volume of production needed to maintain "full employment" of resources (and, in particular, of labor). This perspective generated an attitude toward governmental economic policy that emphasized the government's alleged ability to manipulate monetary and fiscal policy variables so as to ensure full employment. Ludwig von Mises adopted a vigorously dissenting stance toward this Keynesian economics. Although he rarely offered frontal rebuttal to Keynesian theory, his contributions to the topics dealt with in this chapter constituted a well-developed (if implicit) basis for his rejection of Keynesianism.[32] This basis differed, at least in part, from the neoclassical orthodoxy which preceded Keynes (and which Keynes chose to call "classical"); it also differed from the late-twentieth-century neoclassical approaches that have, to a large extent, replaced the Keynesian orthodoxy of earlier decades.

Although we cannot offer here a nuanced account of the differences between Mises' positions and those of his Keynesian and non-Keynesian fellow economists, a few general remarks on these issues may usefully conclude the present chapter. Certainly, Mises rejected (as other economists in the Austrian tradition have rejected) a "macroeconomic" emphasis upon interacting aggregates. Moreover, given his understanding of the dynamic ("disequilibrium") character of the market process (the entrepreneurially competitive process discussed in chapter 4), Mises was unconcerned with the possibility of a chronic ("equilibrium") inadequacy of aggregate demand that might be responsible for systematic, large-scale unemployment. As noted in this chapter, Mises found the causes of business crises (and thus of the bouts of unemployment which typically accompany them) not in inadequate demand, but in the unsustainable projects initiated during booms as a result of artificially low rates of interest caused by monetary expansion. For Mises, what tends to ensure fullest feasible levels of production (and thus of resource employment) is the dynamism of the entrepreneurial market process. It turns out, then, that the Keynesian and similar programs calling for such policies as budgetary deficits (insofar as these must entail monetary expansion), expanded size of the governmental sector of the economy, and manipulation of prices of all kinds (especially including minimum wage laws and manipulation of the interest rate as a policy tool) were seen by Mises as policies likely to exacerbate, rather than to alleviate, cyclical volatility in capitalist systems.

For the concluding three or four decades of his life, which coincided with the heyday of Keynesian influence, Mises was often considered simply old-fashioned and obstinately ortho- dox in his resolute resistance to the brave new economic policies advanced in the post–World War II years. In fact he was consis- tently adhering to a set of theories the subtleties of which were simply not appreciated in the avalanche of the new Keynesian orthodoxy. As we now enter the twenty-first century, we en- counter a more sensitive openness in the economics profession to the advantages of entrepreneurial competition within an in- stitutional framework of secure individual rights. It is to be hoped and anticipated that the ideas of Ludwig von Mises on money, cycles, and interest may now evoke fresh consideration, and perhaps fuller and more sympathetic understanding, than they received during his own lifetime—and especially during his declining years.

CHAPTER SIX

MISES: FREE-MARKET ECONOMIST OF THE CENTURY

THIS CONCLUDING CHAPTER offers an outline of an aspect of Mises' economics that is, in one sense, the most important aspect of all. Indeed, it is this aspect which probably identifies, for many observers, the position occupied by Mises in twentieth-century economics: for better or for worse, Mises is best known not so much as an outstanding economic theorist, not so much for his central role in the development of twentieth-century Austrian economics, but as the most outspoken, most trenchant, and most passionate defender of free-market capitalism—of laissez-faire—of the twentieth century. This chapter will present certain elements in Mises' economics that have not been covered in any of the preceding chapters. But it will also pull together certain implications of a number of topics that were dealt with in earlier chapters in order to help us understand the basis for the strong positions which Mises took regarding central governmental planning (socialism) and governmental intervention into an otherwise free-market economy.

It is important, for the purposes of this book, to bring these implications together for two distinct reasons. First, in the last analysis, these implications have, more than other aspects of his work, decisively shaped Mises' lifework and its public influence. Second, these implications throw significant light on some otherwise overlooked aspects of the substance of his scientific economics. To best appreciate what we mean in this latter regard, it may be useful to confront directly an apparent puzzle in Mises' strong statements in favor of laissez-faire economic policy.

Mises, **Wertfreiheit,** *and the Scientific Case for the Free Market*

We saw at the end of chapter 3 that Mises was emphatic in endorsing Max Weber's doctrine of *wertfreiheit.* Weber had shown the dangers for social scientists of failing to maintain a careful separation between their objective, impartial statements in their role as scientists, on the one hand, and their personal ("nonscientific") beliefs, values, and preferences, on the other. Mises (unlike a number of economists who were otherwise highly sympathetic to his economics) thoroughly agreed. Economics, he insisted, "is perfectly neutral with regard to all judgments of value...." Although economics is, he stated, "the foundation of politics and of every kind of political action," it itself is "apolitical" (HA, 884 f). Whether one is made happy or unhappy by the conclusions of economics does not affect the validity of these conclusions. And these scientific conclusions should not be presented in a manner that might suggest that they *did* make the economist happy (or otherwise).

Now economists have struggled, at least for a century, to spell out the philosophical guidelines that can enable us to translate strictly positive statements of scientific economics into normative guides for policy makers in a way that can invest such normative advice with the authority of science. Value-free medical science research can lead to sound, lifesaving, medical advice. Value-free economic science should be able similarly to generate sound economic policy advice. But the history of economics shows how elusive is the goal of justifying the scientific character of such policy advice.

Out of the attempts to provide such justification has emerged a vast literature dealing with the foundation of what is called *welfare economics.* The classical economists had believed that appropriate economic policy could be identified as that which could increase the "*wealth*" of a nation. When neoclassical economists, toward the close of the nineteenth century, revealed the subtleties and pitfalls which surrounded attempts to pinpoint the meaning of the term, "an increase in the wealth of a nation," they were compelled to seek a substitute criterion. A good deal of neoclassical welfare economics assessed the "goodness" of policy in terms of its ability to increase the "economic *welfare*" of a nation. A dominant strand of twentieth-century welfare economics has believed it possible to judge policy in terms of its impact on the *efficiency* with which a society allocates its scarce resources. But for Austrian economics, none of these attempts can be judged as adequate. The subjectivism of Austrian economics reveals how unsatisfactory it is to work with any notion of aggregate, objective wealth as a policy maximand. (In this, Austrians were thoroughly in tune with their colleagues in other neoclassical schools of economic thought.) Similarly, however, the methodological individualism of Austrian economics renders any notion of aggregate social well-being (of the sort the British neoclassicals—Marshall and Pigou—had developed) to be thoroughly suspect. For similar reasons (as well as for other very important "knowledge" considerations raised by Hayek) Austrians have rejected the idea of social efficiency as a meaningful, relevant yardstick with which to assess the economic goodness of public policy. But all this offers Austrians a most serious challenge. If we lack a scientific standard by which to recognize economic success or economic failure, what *can* we, as scientists rather than political advocates, say about socialism, for example, or about interventionism, without violating the professional standard of *wertfreiheit,* that Mises had so thoroughly accepted as his own? How could Mises, in his role as objective scientist (as distinct from his political position as a classical liberal) denounce governmental price-fixing? How could he denounce central bank inflation of the money supply? How could he denounce government antitrust policy? or protectionism?

Mises, Science, and Economic Goodness

Mises never did explore in any detail the difficulties surrounding the translation of positive economic science into policy advice. He appeared to believe that the economic goodness or badness of a policy could, if the relevant economic theory is thoroughly understood, easily be recognized. Several strands of reasoning in this regard seem to have been taken for granted by Mises. Once we understand the existence and operation of economic "law," and the possibly counter-intuitive outcomes explained by such "law," Mises believed, we can immediately recognize that policy makers (who have instituted economic policies *without* understanding such economic "law") are likely unwittingly to set in motion, through their policies, chains of economic causation which generate outcomes entirely different from (even opposite) *those aimed at by the policy makers themselves.* (It was this likelihood, Mises believed, that explains the tendency for politicians to *deny* the teachings of economics. No one welcomes a science which purports to tell one that one is acting foolishly. It is much easier to endorse intellectual efforts to discredit economic science.) At any rate, Mises believed, we have here clear identification of one kind of "bad" economic policy. A policy is "bad" not because it produces results which the *economists,* as citizens, do not like, but because it leads to results at variance with the objectives *aimed at for that policy by the policy makers themselves.*

A second criterion for judging the economic goodness or badness of a policy is the possibility or impossibility of the successful completion of the plans which that policy encourages. As we saw in the preceding chapter, Mises believed that the central bank inflation that feeds the boom phase of the business cycle does so by encouraging producers to undertake projects that it will be impossible to complete (because these projects, based on "falsely" low money rates of interest, call for sacrifices of consumer goods that the public is in fact not prepared to make). The inflationary policy is thus "bad" economic policy because it encourages plans that are doomed to failure. As we shall see, Mises' criticism of the economic performance of a socialist economy involves his demonstration of the *impossibility* of central planning (in a sense that will be made clear below). Socialism is *not* a "good" economic system; it is predicated on the feasibility of an undertaking (central planning) that is in fact impossible to implement. A policy is "bad" not because economists, as citizens, do not like it, but because it generates plans by individual entrepreneur-producers that they will find impossible to complete.

There appears to be yet a third important basis upon which Mises may have implicitly judged the goodness or badness of economic policy. This has to do with the idea of "consumer sovereignty." As we noticed in chapter 4, Mises believed, *as a proposition of positive economics,* that, with certain exceptions, market outcomes are determined by consumer preferences. Decisions by producers and by resource owners are, in a free-market society, motivated by the desire to anticipate the spending decisions of consumers. (To say that free markets are subject to consumer sovereignty is not to say that free markets "maximize social efficiency," or "maximize aggregate social utility." It is merely to say that all changes in production decisions, all changes in the pattern of resource allocation, are changes calculated—by those decision makers with the most to gain by correct decision making—to take account of consumer preferences, as expressed in their spending decisions.) There are grounds for believing that, in his criticism of what he judged to be unsound economic policies, Mises was simply assuming that his readers held consumer sovereignty to be a desirable feature in an economic system. To show that government intervention frustrates consumer sovereignty is thus to convince these readers that such intervention is, in *their* view, to be deplored. An economic policy is "bad," not because economists, in their capacity as citizens, do not like it, but because it tends to encourage decisions by prospective producers which do not pay all possible regard to the changing patterns of consumer preference.

We can now understand how Mises came to believe that economic science leads us ineluctably to the conclusion that a policy favoring unfettered free markets, a policy of laissez-faire, of capitalism without any government intervention, is scientifically demonstrated to be the best policy. A free market works in a systematic way to encourage coordination among the decisions of market participants, with the motivating force being the needs and preferences of consumers. "The coordination of the autonomous actions of all individuals is accomplished by the operation of the market" (HA, 725). A free market will tend to generate decisions that *can* be successfully implemented and which respect and *do* express consumer sovereignty. If policy makers understand the economics of the free market, their pursuit of laissez-faire will produce results consistent with their expectations, results that will represent successfully completed decisions by market participants, and results that will represent the sovereignty of the consumers. On the other hand, Mises was convinced, intervention by the state can only frustrate the achievement of such results. The most extreme form of state intervention is, of course, the form of economic organization called socialism. And, as we saw in earlier chapters, Mises threw down the gauntlet, with regard to the economics of socialism, as early as 1920. Throughout his life Mises was to consider his work in regard to the possibility or impossibility of central economic planning under socialism to be among the most important of his entire career.

The Economics of Socialism

Mises' theoretical challenge to the possibility of central socialist planning was presented (in a social science journal, *Archiv für Sozialwissenschaft und Sozialpolitik*) under the title "Die Wirtschaftsrechnung im Sozialistischen Gemeinwesen" in 1920—a time when socialism was, to put it mildly, being very seriously advocated in post-World War I Austria. The article was included, with some revisions, in his important 1922 book-length study of the economic and sociological aspects of socialism, and was translated into English in 1935, when it was included in a book, edited by Hayek, entitled *Collectivist Economic Planning: Critical Studies of the Possibilities of Socialism*. Mises' article and book initiated a celebrated debate among economists, one that is still continuing, in fact, to this very day. Mises' critique of the possibility of central socialist planning was grounded in his emphasis upon the most fundamental of economic insights, the role of *economic calculation*.

The foundation of economic efficiency, Mises pointed out, is the rational calculation of benefits and costs, the rational weighing of alternatives. Such calculation is straightforward for the simple conditions under which a Robinson Crusoe must operate. But it becomes much more complicated under less simple conditions. To "choose whether we shall use a waterfall to produce electricity or extend coal-mining and better utilize the energy contained in coal, is quite another matter. Here the processes of production are so many and so long, the conditions necessary to the success of the undertaking so multitudinous, that we can never be content with vague ideas. To decide whether an undertaking is sound we must calculate carefully" (s, 114).

Such calculation cannot, of course, be conducted in terms of heterogeneous physical units (of alternative inputs and/or outputs); such calculation must be conducted in terms of common units of *value*. Under market conditions such units of value are furnished by the money prices that prevail. Calculation using such market prices as the basis for comparison is certainly not perfect, Mises recognized; but its imperfections are sufficiently tolerable for entrepreneur-producers under capitalism to engage in calculative, rational decision making. Mises did not, in asserting the possibility of calculative decision making under capitalism, claim that such decision making conduces to a social optimum. He merely pointed out the possibility of rational individual decision making. Capitalism is based on individual plans (and on their market interaction); such plans are constrained, within the limits of market conditions, to be rational. In contrast, Mises argued, the rational basis for central planning under socialism (that central planning which is, under socialism, intended to replace the independent decisions of individual capitalist producers) is simply absent. There are no indicators of value that might serve as the basis for economic calculation by would-be central planners. "The theory of economic calculation," Mises concluded, "shows that in the socialistic community economic calculation would be impossible" (s, 131).

Mises' contention rests on the circumstance that, by definition, *the socialistic community does not include a market for resource services.* Money prices for *consumer goods* might be imagined for the socialist economy. "But since the prices of the various factors of production (including labor) could not be expressed in money, money could play no part in economic calculations" (s, 121). Production decisions can be *calculated* decisions only if the decision makers can assign *values* to units of resources (based on their potential usefulness in alternative available processes of production). But would-be socialist planners have no market-generated money factor prices available to them. Their decision-making must be made, in effect, in physical terms, something utterly inconsistent with rational economic planning with regard to resource allocation.[1] Rational central planning, under socialism, is simply impossible.

It should be emphasized that, in declaring socialist central planning to be an impossibility, Mises was not declaring it impossible for a socialist economy to exist—even for a period of decades. He was not at all disturbed by the circumstance that the Soviet Union's existence was a protracted one. He was merely declaring it impossible for the decisions made in such an economy to be "rational," i.e., to be consistent with the priorities that the planners themselves wish to maintain. A socialist economy can continue to "exist" even when the goods produced are not the ones which the planners prefer (over alternatives that might have been produced). A socialist economy can continue to "exist" even when resources are used in wasteful fashion (i.e., in ways that result in fewer of the desired bundles of consumer goods than might have been achieved by a more rational allocation pattern). But clearly a socialist economy, without the possibility of rational economic calculation, is doomed to inefficiency and thus, at least relatively, to poverty and stunted growth. The poverty in which the masses lived in the Soviet Union was something that Mises' theory explained superbly well. Mises dealt a devastating blow to the illusion that the extraordinary record of economic growth in capitalist economies during the preceding century, the dramatic rises in standards of living in Western market-based societies, could be duplicated without a market for resource services. Mises showed socialism, insofar as it had been proposed as an *economic* system of organization, to be an utter failure.

No account of the remarkable (and quite fierce!) debate among economists that was initiated by Mises' critique can be provided here.[2] I do, however, wish to emphasize that Mises' argument was based solidly on his "Austrian" understanding of the market. This understanding (as we saw in chapter 4) sees the market not as a system somehow yielding instantaneous equilibrium patterns of resource allocation, but as a continuous process in which dynamic price and quality competition between producer-entrepreneurs is (on the basis of the perceived pure profit opportunities inherent at each moment in the continually changing arrays of market prices) continually modifying patterns of resource allocation so as better to anticipate consumer preferences. The resource market prices which are lacking under socialism cannot, in this understanding, be replaced by centrally promulgated (nonmarket) "prices" on the basis of which "calculation" can be conducted. (Misunderstanding on this score was responsible for significant confusion in the debate which followed Mises' 1920 paper.[3] To understand Mises' criticism of the socialist economy one must first understand his appreciation of the dynamic, entrepreneurially competitive character of the market economy.) But Mises' reasoning on behalf of the capitalist market economy was not confined to his powerful critique of its socialist alternative. Mises was convinced that economic prosperity requires not simply a market economy. He believed that prosperity calls for a market economy that is in no way "hampered" by the kinds of government intervention which have in fact characterized Western capitalist countries during the twentieth century.

The Mixed Economy: The Impossibility
of a Stable "Third Way"

Mises was well aware of the political attractiveness of interventionism as economic policy. If socialism was the most serious threat in the immediate post–World War I years, interventionism was the enduring twentieth-century danger for capitalism. Especially after its disastrous experience of the depression during the thirties, public opinion in Western capitalist economies clamored for regulation, controls, and other forms of direct or indirect government intervention in markets—in order, as the public saw it, to protect against the hazards and/or excesses of laissez-faire. Politicians catering to this widespread demand for proactive governmental economic policy (especially in the years of the so-called Keynesian revolution) offered economic programs seeking to offer the best of both worlds: the advantages of free-market capitalism with the perceived protections of centrally planned fiscal, monetary, and market regulation. Textbooks on economic principles taught millions of students that the mixed economy was the virtually unanimous choice of enlightened modern economists. Mises would have none of this.

Mises believed that the idea of a mixed economy as a viable "third way" was simply a myth. And, he emphasized, he believed this idea to be an entirely dangerous myth. Mises' intellectual onslaught against interventionism goes back at least to the twenties.[4] But it was especially during the last decades of his life that Mises devoted himself to developing his critique of interventionism. Among the targets of Mises' scathing criticism were virtually all the manifestations of the interventionist program: antitrust policy, price controls of all kinds (with perhaps especial emphasis on minimum wage laws and rent controls), inflationary monetary policy, budgetary deficits, farm subsidies, tariff protection, nationalization of foreign-owned companies, income and wealth transfers, and on and on. All the programs that make up what is euphemistically termed the "modern welfare state" came under his withering attack.

All of these interventionist policies, Mises pointed out, are either doomed to failure—because they fly in the face of consumer preferences and will thus fail to achieve their objectives—or will generate unwelcome results not at all intended by the policy makers themselves. Minimum wage legislation (and "pro-union" legislation interfering with the competitive process of the labor market) will yield unemployment (EFI, 29, 67, 71). Legislation aimed at the large size of major business firms (or their high concentration within industries) will raise costs to the consuming public (EFI, 208). Inflationary monetary policy generates slumps (EFI, 107), and hurts the public, particularly the poor, who own savings and other assets (EFI, 34 f, 103 f, 188 ff); eventually such policy can lead to hyperinflation (EFI, 83). Keynesian full employment policy invariably turns out to be inflationary, with all its unfortunate results (EFI, 76-81). U.S. farm policy has led to the farmer's complete loss of economic independence (EFI, 208 f). Inheritance taxes encourage precisely the kind of concentration in business that interventionists profess to oppose (EFI, 210).

But the worst result of interventionist policies is that they lead inevitably to further and further government control of the economy. Interventionism is a slippery slope leading to socialism. Again and again Mises dismissed the idea of a viable, stable economic system that is neither one of socialist planning nor one of capitalist free enterprise. There is, Mises argued, a built-in dynamic in a regime of government intervention that inevitably sets in motion a systematic series of changes leading in the direction of complete socialism.[5] By "government intervention" Mises was referring to "interference with the market" (EP, 40), to governmental activities or decrees which force "the entrepreneurs and capitalists to employ some of the factors of production in a way different from what they would have resorted to if they were only obeying the dictates of the market" (HA, 718). The form of socialism to which the interventionist system is tending is what Mises called the "Hindenburg pattern of socialism" (HA, 723), one in which *nominal* features of a market economy (such as private property ownership, prices, wages, and interest rates) are retained but in which in fact market participants "are bound to obey unconditionally the orders issued by the government's supreme office of production management" (HA, 717).

The reason why this dynamic renders a system of interventionism unstable is that acts of intervention tend to produce results "which—from the point of view of their own advocates and the governments resorting to them—are more unsatisfactory than the previous state of affairs which they were designed to alter" (EFI, 55). A philosophy that sustains interventionism as a way of dealing with apparently undesirable features of the economy will then tend to generate new acts of intervention in order to deal with the unfortunate results of the earlier acts of intervention. Thus, governments who find certain commodity market prices to be "too high," are tempted to impose price ceilings. Such price ceilings, simple economics predicts, tend to produce commodity shortages. To cope with these shortages (and the arbitrariness of resulting patterns of consumption) the government is likely to impose rationing, and/or to extend price controls to the resource markets, etc.[6]

It should be noted that in criticizing the interventionist program (and in declaring illusionary the idea that the interventionist system could be a stable alternative to both socialism and laissez-faire capitalism), Mises emphasized that he did not at all deny the need for, and a proper role for, government. Unlike some of his followers,[7] Mises did not at all question the need for government, and this was with full awareness of all its coercive apparatus "for violent prevention and suppression of antisocial action on the part of refractory individuals and groups of individuals" (HA, 719).[8] Mises was no anarchist; he did not even see the government as a "necessary evil" to be minimized (EFI, 57). He saw government, with its function of protecting private property rights, as an essential prerequisite for the free-market society. Government, he emphasized, is a *beneficial* institution in that it makes possible the cooperative achievements of the market. The political problem presented for all eras, however, is that this valuable institution is vulnerable to the danger of becoming tyrannical and totalitarian. In our time, in addition, such danger has extended to more subtle and more powerful forms, in that it is obscured and disguised by the illusion that interference with the market sovereignty of consumers is somehow in the economic interest of the public. This is the source of the willingness of the public to endorse expansions in the role of government, beyond its valuable and necessary function of ensuring the inviolability of property rights, to outright interference in the way such property rights are deployed in free markets. Such interference, Mises was convinced, necessarily tends to undermine those powerful but sensitive webs of interpersonal cause-and-effect that we call the market process. A policy of interventionism is, in effect, a policy to replace the market by the state.

Mises did not hesitate to express his views on interventionism even where they seemed to put him at odds with his most admired and influential intellectual allies. Friedrich Hayek, whom we saw to be one of Mises' strongest supporters in his critique of socialism, published his celebrated *Constitution of Liberty* in 1960. Mises reviewed this work and termed it a "great book," providing "a brilliant exposition of the meaning of liberty and the creative powers of a free civilization" (EFI, 151 f). Yet Mises pulled no punches in expressing his disappointment with Hayek's treatment, in that book, of a number of features of the welfare state. "In fact," Mises wrote, "the Welfare State is merely a method for transforming the market economy step by step into socialism" (EFI, 151). Indeed, Mises continued, Hayek's own "searching analysis of the policies and concerns of the Welfare State" cannot fail to convey how these policies must fail to achieve their designed objectives, inducing "further acts of intervention...until all economic freedom has been virtually abolished. What emerges is the system of all-round planning, i.e., socialism of the type which the German Hindenburg plan was aiming at in the first World War and which was later put into effect by Hitler after his seizure of power and by the British Coalition Cabinet in the Second World War" (EFI, 152).

Mises, Economics, and Classical Liberalism

Mises' convictions concerning the *economic* goodness of laissez-faire capitalism were separate from, but closely linked to, his own advocacy of classical liberalism as a *political* program. Throughout his career as an economist Mises insisted on the objective, nonpolitical, impartial character of his science, and yet he also passionately believed in and advocated (as a nonscientific, value-laden ideal) the political program of classical liberalism.[9] At times, Mises may have *seemed* to ignore the distinction between his science and his political convictions; the truth is that the distinction is indeed a subtle one, yet one which Mises articulated with great precision. "Liberalism...is a political doctrine. It is not a theory, but an application of the theories developed...especially by economics to definite problems of human action within society." Economic science is value-neutral, but "as a political doctrine liberalism is not neutral with regard to values and the ultimate ends sought by action. It assumes that all men or at least the majority of people are intent upon attaining certain goals....While...economics...uses the terms happiness and removal of uneasiness in a purely formal sense, liberalism attaches to them a concrete meaning" (HA, 153 f).

The distinction between classical liberalism and economics is an especially subtle one for Mises because he saw the former as a direct application of the scientific conclusions of the latter. Economics, for Mises, teaches that free markets permit and enable participating individuals to achieve their own goals through mutual cooperation and exchange. These teachings, Mises maintained, were first developed as "scientific theory without any thought of its political significance" (LCT, 195). The ideology of liberalism that was *derived* from this positive theory applied the theory to develop a political program through which man in society may act to achieve his goals, insofar as man is presumed to "prefer life to death, health to sickness, nourishment to starvation, abundance to poverty" (HA, 154).

The closeness between Mises' liberalism and his economics expresses Mises' *utilitarian* perspective. Liberalism deploys the teachings of economics to articulate its political program. But for Mises the teachings of economics seem inevitably to lead (on utilitarian grounds) to that very political program. "One cannot understand liberalism without a knowledge of economics. For liberalism is applied economics; it is social and political policy based on a scientific foundation" (LCT, 195). As William Baumgarth explained, Mises sought to offer a theory of society that is as value-free as conceivably possible. For Mises, classical liberalism does not *need* to depend, for its moral force, upon the asserted ethical imperatives of such categories as freedom or justice; its moral force flows out of economic understanding as it relates to the actual motives of men in society, whatever they may be. Mises' "attempt to offer such a theory was a bold one and went as far in the direction of utilitarianism as perhaps it is possible to go."[10] Baumgarth himself had serious doubts as to the moral *persuasiveness* of a political program which avoids ethically imperative reference to categories such as "justice" and "honor." Yet it is quite certain that for Mises, the ideal he constructed virtually purely from his economic science provided an ideology sufficiently heady to invest his entire career with a passion and sense of dedication rarely to be found in scientific work. Indeed, there is no doubt that the passion Mises poured into his scientific work derived in large measure from his awareness of its relevance to the political program he believed flowed from it.

Although we do not have any published writings expressing Mises' classical liberal outlook before his 1919 *Nation, State and Economy*, we can surmise that he imbibed this outlook much earlier, during his years of immersion in the pre–World War I Austrian School.[11] In his monograph *The Historical Setting of the Austrian School of Economics*, published when he was eighty-eight years of age, Mises revealed a good deal of the political context of the *methodenstreit* which raged around the turn of the century and earlier between the Austrian School and the German Historical School. One can sense in Mises' language and references the moral contempt with which he (and presumably the early Austrians) viewed the professors of the German School, and his conviction that the political loyalties of these professors and their followers led directly from their roles as the "intellectual bodyguard of the House of Hohenzollern"[12] to their becoming supporters of the Nazis after World War I (HSAS, 32). It was in Bismarck's Germany that the government inaugurated "its *Sozialpolitik*, the system of interventionist measures such as labor legislation, social security, pro-union attitudes, progressive taxation, protective tariffs, cartels and dumping" (HSAS, 30). The German Historical School provided the intellectual ammunition for these policies. Its political influence "consisted in the fact that it rendered Germany safe for the ideas, the acceptance of which made popular with the German people all those disastrous policies that resulted in the great catastrophes. The aggressive imperialism that twice ended in war and defeat, the limitless inflation of the early Twenties, the *Zwangswirtschaft* and all the horrors of the Nazi regime were achievements of politicians who acted as they had been taught by the champions of the Historical School" (HSAS, 31). Mises clearly identified himself with what he called "the liberalism of the Austrian economists" who rejected the German Historical School (HSAS, 34).

In the American environment of the 1940s in which Mises found himself upon his arrival in his new country, and in the immediate postwar years, Mises was, as was noted in chapter 1, often considered a "conservative." He was a staunch opponent of the social measures which had been introduced by Franklin D. Roosevelt in the wake of the depression of the 1930s; he was unflagging in his opposition to the Keynesian fiscal and monetary policies that acquired enormous popularity during those years. With both major U.S. political parties supporting these interventionist measures (with greater or lesser degrees of enthusiasm, or with greater or lesser degrees of comprehensiveness), Mises found himself not merely out of step with prevailing fashions in economic policy; he found himself treated as an extremely (perhaps absurdly) conservative figure, one vainly attempting to restore a laissez-faire regime that had been decisively rejected, both intellectually and politically, decades earlier. And it is true that Mises found support among men and organizations associated with the "rock-ribbed" conservative wing of the Republican Party. Yet Mises never did see himself as a conservative; he was outspoken in his explicit identification of (classical) liberalism as his own political ideology. It is ironic but significant that in the semantic confusions of his time, those who in the U.S. termed themselves "liberals" (appropriating the term from the classical liberals in order to describe their own interventionist program—the very opposite of the position held by the classical liberals) were seen by Mises as following precisely those statist, conservative-authoritarian policies and philosophies against which the champions of his own classical liberalism had, in an earlier age, been radical rebels.[13] Leland Yeager has accurately described Mises' position: "Mises was emphatically not a conservative. His book [the 1919 *Nation, State and Economy*] rails repeatedly against political and economic privilege. He championed political democracy as well as a free-market economy. He admired democratic revolutions against hereditary and authoritarian regimes...."[14]

Economics, Austrian Economics, and the Case for the Free Market

Both fervent proponents and fierce critics of free-market capitalism have often pointed out the obvious relevance of neoclassical economics (the economics which has, for a good part of the twentieth century, been understood as the economic orthodoxy) for the defense of capitalism. Marxists and other critics of free-market capitalism have never ceased to denounce neoclassical economics, with the standard theory of market price as its core, precisely because that economics appears to provide powerful ammunition for asserting the economic efficiency of the capitalist system. George Stigler, associated with a far more benign appreciation of capitalism, has pointed out that, as compared with other fields of social science, economics tends to instil in its practitioners a generally less skeptical (and often in fact a more favorable) attitude toward the achievements of the market.[15] It is neoclassical economics which seems to demonstrate the benign power of Adam Smith's "invisible hand" to generate prices and allocate resources in systematic, and apparently desirable, fashion. In order to argue any economic failures in capitalism it is clearly necessary to undermine the core teachings of neoclassical economics, or, at any rate, to challenge the relevance of its well-behaved theoretical models to the complex realities of the world in which we must live.

It must seem surprising, then, to discover that during much of the twentieth century, it was orthodox economics itself that was made to serve as the intellectual basis for the widespread interventionism that has characterized the century (and especially the decades coinciding with and immediately following Mises' arrival in the U.S.). What explains this apparent paradox is that economists did indeed challenge the relevance of the neoclassical models to the real world.

The real world, many economists argued, unlike the neoclassical theoretical world, is a world of imperfect competition, a world pervaded by externalities, a world rendered unstable by the volatility and possible inadequacy of aggregate demand. This stance allowed economists to pay some lip-service to the elegance of the orthodox models, while at the same time insisting on the need for government interventions to deal with the problems, rampant in the real world, for which the orthodox models had no explanation and no solution. The growth of interventionism as a political ideology was thus parallel to the trend within the economics profession to use the "unrealism" of its models to demonstrate the *shortcomings* of free-market capitalism. To Ludwig von Mises these developments made no sense at all. A convincing case can be made that what enabled Mises to resist the fashionability of the interventionist economics of his time was the uniquely *Austrian* character of his own economics.

The truth is that the Austrian tradition that Mises had received and that he extended and deepened never did accept as central those rarefied models of perfectly competitive equilibrium that the midcentury critics of laissez-faire capitalism deployed to demonstrate that system's real-world shortcomings. As we saw in chapter 4, Mises worked with a theoretical construct that focused upon dynamic entrepreneurial competition in a world of disequilibrium. It was in the context of this dynamically competitive process—rather than in the unrealistic perfectly competitive equilibrium models of midcentury neoclassical microeconomics—that Mises saw the benign market process at work. It was this process, a process at work no less in the area of the monetary sector of the market than in the real sector, which Mises believed to constrain resource prices and resource allocation patterns, interest rates, and the value of money, to take account of hitherto overlooked (or unanticipated) changes in consumer preferences.

There is no contradiction between this disequilibrium framework of Mises' Austrian economics and the facts of the real world. The lessons Mises learned regarding the achievements of the free market emphatically *did* apply to the world for which public policy must be formulated. For Mises, in order to understand the relevance of the theory of the market process to the defense of free-market capitalism, it was not necessary to extend the technical sophistication of market models; it was simply necessary to appreciate the subtleties of the market process itself. The logic of economic reasoning in the 1950s and the 1960s was no different from, and had lost none of its real world relevance in comparison to, the economic reasoning of the 1920s. For Mises, the economists of the postwar years had disastrously lost their way. In fact, it seemed to him that it was the very advances in the technical sophistication of midcentury economics that were to blame for this tragic misuse of the science. It was this which drove Mises, during the last decades of his career, to attempt again and again to clarify what he believed to be the true epistemological and methodological foundations of economics.

Mises: The Free-Market Economist of the Century

Few will argue with the judgment that, in terms of the vigor and passion with which he attacked socialist and interventionist alternatives to laissez-faire capitalism, Ludwig von Mises was the foremost economist of the twentieth century.[16] What we have seen is that in thus defying the conventional policy wisdom of his century, Mises was simply articulating the straightforward implications of his own strictly scientific contributions to the positive, objective discipline of pure economics. Both in his positive economics and in his policy positions, Mises was virtually alone. He watched with sadness twentieth-century developments both in economics and in the public policy fashions sweeping the nominally capitalist societies of the West. "The public discussion of economic problems ignores almost entirely all that has been said by economists in the last two hundred years. Prices, wage rates, interest rates and profits are treated as if their determination were not subject to any law. Governments try to decree and to enforce maximum commodity prices and minimum wage rates. Statesmen exhort businessmen to cut down profits, to lower prices, and to raise wages as if these matters were dependent on the laudable intentions of individuals. In the treatment of international economic relations people blithely resort to the most naïve fallacies of Mercantilism. Few are aware of the shortcomings of all these popular doctrines, or realize why the policies based upon them invariably spread disaster" (HA, 879 f).

Mises could suggest only one way to combat these "sad facts": "by never relaxing in the search for truth" (HA, 880). Mises' entire career as an economist—from his Vienna days as a brilliant young scholar and as one deeply involved in the hectic world of post–World War I public policy, to his years in Geneva as a renowned senior scholar, to his three decades of lonely, unfashionable teaching and writing in the U.S during his old age—represented Mises' extraordinary, courageous, sustained fulfillment of this ideal. He never faltered in his belief that the "body of economic knowledge is an essential element in the structure of human civilization; it is the foundation upon which modern industrialism and all the moral, intellectual, technological, and therapeutical achievements of the last centuries have been built" (HA, 885). Mises persisted "in the search for truth" in the face of the disdainful dismissal of his work by the professional economics establishment of his time because he saw his work as essential for the preservation of human civilization.

At the dawn of the twenty-first century, there is reason to believe that the work of the foremost free-market economist of the twentieth century will not be forgotten.

MISESIAN ECONOMICS
AFTER MISES

THE CENTRAL PURPOSE of this work has been to set forth, in outline, the economic thought of Ludwig von Mises. The story of Mises' economics ends, in one sense, with the conclusion of Mises' life. And the story we have told in this book is therefore, in this sense, ended. But there is of course another sense in which the story of Mises' economics has continued to unfold *after* his death. Although our own purpose has not been to tell the story of the impact which Mises' work has had upon late-twentieth-century economic thought, we must certainly, in doing justice to Mises' contributions, take brief note of the remarkable resurgence of Austrian Economics that has occurred since 1973. That resurgence has consisted primarily in the rediscovery of the vitality and cogency of Mises' ideas.

During a period in which the mainstream of economic theorizing has pursued the path of formal, technical sophistication, many younger economists, disenchanted with the aridity and artificiality of the model-building approach, have found intellectual stimulation and satisfaction in Mises' relatively simple, but powerful and fundamental, insights. After decades during which the need for and value of government intervention in the market economy were the unquestioned bases of public policy, after decades during which socialism was admired as a viable and morally attractive alternative to "unbridled" capitalism, Misesian views concerning the economic incoherence of socialism—and the case for complete, or virtually complete, laissez-faire—have somehow become part and parcel of respectable public policy discourse. (Certainly these latter developments can, in great part, be attributed also to other intellectual currents, as well as historical and political changes which extend far beyond the direct scope of Mises' economics.)[1]

Karen Vaughn has recently described this revival. As she points out, there would have been little doubt among economists in 1974 (the year after Mises' death) "that the Austrian school was a closed chapter in the history of economics." But it is today obvious that such predictions were sorely mistaken. "Austrian concerns such as imperfect information, time and market coordination are now part and parcel of modern economics.... Even more surprising, articles devoted to research from an overtly Austrian perspective now routinely find their way into respectable, if not elite, academic journals. Mainstream

publishers...are all publishing books about the Austrian school....
There are institutes and programmes named after both Mises
and Hayek on both sides of the Atlantic...."[2]

Mises may not have agreed with a good deal of the "new"
Austrian economics. Many of the new Austrian economists came
to question specific parts of the Misesian system. But there can
be no doubt that the prime moving element responsible for the
resurgence of the Austrian tradition was the impact of the work
of Mises himself. Sometimes Mises' disciples have disagreed
among themselves regarding Mises' views on specific issues, or
regarding the interpretation to be placed on some of his more
cryptic statements. Some followers of Mises have, with more
than a hint of aggressiveness, believed themselves to be more
"pure" Misesians than others. Some followers of Mises have learned
to appreciate the complementarities between Mises' own work
and that of his most famous fellow-Austrian, Friedrich Hayek;
others have held that Hayek's work differs radically from that of
his mentor. Out of the debates—sometimes inspiring and intellectually fertile, sometimes disappointing and intellectually dispir-
iting—on these issues, a broad group of scholars has emerged
who are all working within the Austrian tradition, and who
recognize the work of Mises as being the most powerful and
radical expression of that tradition in the twentieth century.

It is notoriously hazardous to predict the future course of
intellectual history. Yet this writer believes that the resurgence

of interest in the Austrian tradition and in the Misesian approach will endure. This does not mean that Misesian positions on method, on markets, on monetary and trade cycle theory, and on capital theory will necessarily command the agreement of future economists. It does not even mean that a live, identifiable Austrian tradition in economics will be a reality in, say, fifty years. It means, rather, that the broad sweep of Mises' view of the workings of the market economy—his focus on human action, on the purposefulness of action, on the entrepreneurial element in the market process, on the subjectivism with which economic understanding must be pursued—will continue to find a place within the menu of intellectual options available in twenty-first-century economics. These themes are too compelling, too persuasive, and too obviously fertile to be lost in the technicalities of any future economics. For the future historian of twenty-first-century economic thought, it will inevitably be necessary to recognize the impact of a remarkable twentieth-century Austrian economist, Ludwig von Mises.

BOOKS BY MISES

THIS LIST includes only English-language works, and it includes only their earliest publication (many of these works have appeared many times in subsequent editions). Where a work is a translation from the German, the date of the earliest German-language original has been provided in square brackets. For full bibliographical information on all books and articles by Mises published before 1993, see Bettina Bien-Greaves and Robert W. McGee, *Mises: An Annotated Bibliography, A Comprehensive Listing of Books and Articles by and about Ludwig von Mises* (Irvington-on-Hudson, N.Y.: The Foundation for Economic Education, 1993).

1. *The Theory of Money and Credit* [1912]. Translated by H. E. Batson. London: Jonathan Cape, 1934.
2. *Nation, State and Economy* [1919]. Translated by Leland B. Yeager. New York: New York University Press, 1983.

3. *Socialism: An Economic and Sociological Analysis* [1922]. Translated by J. Kahane. London: Jonathan Cape, 1936.

4. *The Free and Prosperous Commonwealth: An Exposition of the Ideas of Classical Liberalism* [1927]. Translated by Ralph Raico. Princeton: Van Nostrand, 1962. Later editions were published under the title *Liberalism: In the Classical Tradition*.

5. *A Critique of Interventionism* [1929]. Translated by Hans F. Sennholz. New Rochelle, N.Y.: Arlington House, 1977.

6. *Epistemological Problems of Economics* [1933]. Translated by George Reisman. Princeton: Van Nostrand, 1960.

7. *Omnipotent Government: The Rise of the Total State and Total War*. New Haven: Yale University Press, 1944.

8. *Bureaucracy*. New Haven: Yale University Press, 1944.

9. *Planned Chaos*. Irvington-on-Hudson, N.Y.: Foundation for Economic Education, 1947.

10. *Human Action: A Treatise on Economics*. New Haven: Yale University Press, 1949. This work is a revision, expansion, and translation of an earlier German-language book, *Nationalökonomie: Theorie des Handelns und Wirtschaftens*, Geneva, 1940.

11. *Planning for Freedom, and Other Essays and Addresses*. South Holland, Ill.: Libertarian Press, 1952.

12. *The Anti-Capitalist Mentality*. Princeton: Van Nostrand, 1956.

13. *Theory and History: An Interpretation of Social and Economic Evolution*. New Haven: Yale University Press, 1957.

14. *The Ultimate Foundation of Economic Science: An Essay on Method.* Princeton: Van Nostrand, 1962.

15. *The Historical Setting of the Austrian School of Economics.* New Rochelle, N.Y.: Arlington House, 1969.

Published Posthumously

16. *Notes and Recollections.* Translated by Hans F. Sennholz. South Holland, Ill.: Libertarian Press, 1978.

17. *On the Manipulation of Money and Credit.* Translated by Bettina Bien-Greaves; edited by Percy L. Greaves, Jr. Dobbs Ferry, N.Y.: Free Market Books, 1978. Includes translations of several shorter German-language books published by Mises in 1923, 1928, and 1931.

18. *The Clash of Group Interests and Other Essays.* Edited by Richard M. Ebeling. New York: The Center for Libertarian Studies, 1978.

19. *Economic Policy: Thoughts for Today and Tomorrow.* Edited by Margit von Mises and George Koether. South Bend, Ind.: Regnery/Gateway, 1979. Edited from transcribed tapes of lectures delivered in Argentina, in 1959.

20. *Money, Method and the Market Process: Essays by Ludwig von Mises.* Selected by Margit von Mises; edited by Richard M. Ebeling. Auburn, Ala.: Praxeology Press of the Ludwig von Mises Institute; Norwell, Mass.: Kluwer Academic Publishers, 1990.

21. *Economic Freedom and Interventionism: An Anthology of Articles and Essays.* Selected and edited by Bettina Bien-Greaves. Irvington-on-Hudson, N.Y.: Foundation for Economic Education, 1990.

22. *Selected Writings of Ludwig von Mises: The Political Economy of International Reform and Reconstruction.* Edited by Richard M. Ebeling. Indianapolis: Liberty Fund, 2000.

NOTES

Chapter One

1. I understand that two separate full-length biographies of Mises are now being prepared by Professor Richard Ebeling and by Dr. J. Guido Hülsmann.

2. Carl Menger (1840-1921) was the founder of the Austrian School of Economics. His *Grundsätze der Volkswirthschaftslehre* (1871) was the book which initiated the Austrian tradition.

3. Eugen von Böhm-Bawerk (1851-1914) was one of the founding leaders of the Austrian School of Economics.

4. Although the claims made by Mises (in the quotations in this paragraph) may at first seem immodest, there are at least some grounds for accepting them at face value. See note 6 below.

5. See Jacques Rueff, "The Intransigence of Ludwig von Mises," chapter 1 in *On Freedom and Free Enterprise: Essays in Honor*

of Ludwig von Mises, ed. M. Sennholz, rev. ed. (Irvington-on-Hudson, N.Y.: Foundation for Economic Education, 1994).

6. For confirmation of Mises' crucial role in stemming the Austrian inflation (and for personal information that one of the great disappointments of Mises' life was his not being called at that time to take over the finance ministry to stabilize the currency), see F. A. Hayek, *Hayek on Hayek: An Autobiographical Dialogue,* ed. S. Kresge and L. Wenar (London: Routledge, 1994), 70.

7. *Hayek on Hayek,* 59. See also Earlene Craver, "The Emigration of Austrian Economists," *History of Political Economy* 18 (spring 1987), 5.

8. For Mises' own account of the political events of these years, see NR, chapter 15.

9. See MYWM, 41, for Kelsen's remark on this.

10. In oral remarks Hayek once described (in the presence of this writer) his own trepidation when he first sent Mises a copy of his 1937 *Economica* paper, "Economics and Knowledge," in which he (somewhat obliquely) took issue with certain Misesian positions.

11. *Hayek on Hayek,* 72.

12. Fritz Machlup, "Ludwig von Mises: A Scholar Who Would Not Compromise," in *Homage to Mises: The First Hundred Years,* J. K. Andrews, Jr. (Hillsdale, Mich.: Hillsdale College Press, 1981), 25.

13. Ibid.

14. Ibid., 23.

15. Rueff, "Intransigence of Ludwig von Mises," 15.

16. W. H. Peterson, "Mises and Keynes," in *Homage to Mises,* 30.

17. W. H. Rappard, "On Reading von Mises," in *On Freedom and Free Enterprise,* 17.

18. See Hans F. Sennholz, "Postscript," to NR, 156ff; MYWM, chapter 9.

Chapter Two

1. See *Hayek on Hayek,* 55, where Grünberg is described as "an economic historian who was a socialist and became later the founder of the famous Marxist-Freudian Frankfurt Institute of Social Research."

2. The relationship between Schumpeter and Mises, both personally and professionally, remained somewhat complicated throughout their careers. See further S. Boehm, "The Austrian Tradition: Schumpeter and Mises" (together with "Commentary" by the present writer), in *Neoclassical Economic Theory, 1870-1930,* ed. K. Hennings and W. Samuels, editors, (Boston, Dordrecht, London: Kluwer, 1990).

3. Nikolai Bukharin, "Introduction" [to the Russian edition, 1919] as translated in *The Economic Theory of the Leisure Class* (New York and London: Monthly Review Press, 1972), 9.

4. See 8 in L. von Mises, *Epistemological Problems of Economics* (Princeton, N.J.: Van Nostrand, 1960). This book is the English translation of his *Grundprobleme der Nationalökonomie* (1933); this chapter was first published as a journal article in 1928.

5. See Lionel C. Robbins, "Introduction" (to the 1934 English edition), reprinted in the revised (1953) edition of *Ludwig von Mises, The Theory of Money and Credit* (New Haven: Yale University Press), 12. The translation was of the second (1924) German edition of the work.

6. For some elaboration of these statements see below, chapter 5.

7. Martha Steffy Browne, "Erinnerungen an das Mises-Privatseminar," in *Ludwig von Mises—seine Ideen und seine Wirkung* [this is the title of a special number of *Wirtschaftspolitische Blätter* 1981 (4)], 111.

8. Besides Martha Steffy Browne, Gottfried Haberler wrote a piece "Mises' Private Seminar" in the above-cited number of *Wirtschaftspolitischer Blätter.* See also, the second edition of MYWM (Cedar Falls, Iowa: Center for Futures Education, 1984), appendix 1; also *Hayek on Hayek,* 71.

9. *Hayek on Hayek,* 71f.

10. Haberler, "Mises' Private Seminar," 123.

11. Browne, "Erinnerungen an das Mises-Privatseminar," 120.

12. Stephan Boehm, "Austrian Economics Between the Wars:

Some Historiographical Problems," in *Austrian Economics: Tensions and New Directions,* ed. Bruce J. Caldwell and Stephan Boehm (Boston, Dordrecht, London: Kluwer, 1992), 6ff.

13. L. C. Robbins, *The Nature and Significance of Economic Science,* 2nd edition, (London: Macmillan, 1935), xv. This statement was from the preface to the first edition of the book, 1932.

14. See Fritz Machlup, "Austrian Economics" in *Encyclopedia of Economics,* ed. D. Greenwald (New York: McGraw-Hill, 1982).

15. See V. C. Walsh, *Introduction to Contemporary Microeconomics* (New York: McGraw-Hill, 1970), 17.

16. Murray N. Rothbard, "Ludwig von Mises: The Dean of the Austrian School," in *15 Great Austrian Economists,* ed. R. G. Holcombe (Auburn, Ala.: Ludwig von Mises Institute, 1999), 159.

17. Ibid.

18. *Hayek on Hayek,* 76.

19. Although several writers have claimed that Hayekian economics differs in crucial respects from that of Mises, this writer strongly disagrees. For a discussion of how, despite some significant differences between them, both Mises and Hayek understand the nature of the market process in basically the same non-neoclassical way, see Israel M. Kirzner,

"Reflections on the Misesian Legacy in Economics," *Review of Austrian Economics* 9, no. 2 (1996): 143-54; reprinted as chapter 8 in Israel M. Kirzner, *The Driving Force of the Market: Essays in Austrian Economics* (London and New York: Routledge, 2000). There is every reason to recognize that one of Mises' most important influences upon twentieth-century economics consists in this "Misesian" character of Hayek's understanding of the market process.

20. On this see Frank M. Machovec, *Perfect Competition and the Transformation of Economics* (London and New York: Routledge, 1995).

21. A prominent example of this is Terence W. Hutchison's *The Significance and Basic Postulates of Economic Theory* (London: Macmillan, 1938).

22. Frank H. Knight, "Professor Mises and the Theory of Capital," *Economica* 8 (November 1941): 409.

23. See the citation above, chapter 1, note 8.

24. F. A. Hayek, *The Counter-Revolution of Science: Studies on the Abuse of Reason* (Glencoe: Free Press, 1955), 31.

25. Ibid. 209f.

Chapter Three

1. "Social Science and Natural Science," *Journal of Social Philosophy and Jurisprudence* 7, No. 3 (April 1942); "The Treatment of 'Irrationality' in the Social Sciences," *Philosophy*

and Phenomenological Research 4, no. 4, (June 1944). Both these papers have been republished in MMMP.

2. Mises considered the idea of economic law to be the great contribution of the classical economists. He attached particular importance to what he called the Ricardian "Law of Association" [see HA, 159-64], a generalization of what is more commonly termed the "Law of Comparative Advantage."

3. See his "'What is Truth' in Economics?" *Journal of Political Economy* 48, no. 1 (Feb. 1940), reprinted as chapter 7 in F. H. Knight, *On the History and Method of Economics: Selected Essays* (Chicago: University of Chicago Press, 1956).

4. Roger Koppl, "Alfred Schutz and F. A. Hayek as Misesian Methodologists," (paper delivered to workshop on "Spontaneous Orders: Austrian Economics, Philosophy and Aesthetics," Copenhagen School of Business, November 1998), 4.

5. F. Machlup, *Methodology of Economics and Other Social Sciences* (New York: Academic Press, 1978), ix.

6. "Operationalism" was a notion first advanced by Percy Bridgman in 1927. The doctrine eventually had great influence on midcentury mainstream economics; see for example, P. A. Samuelson, *Foundations of Economic Analysis* (Cambridge: Harvard University Press, 1947); R. G. Lipsey and P. O. Steiner, *Economics* (New York: Harper and Row, 1966).

7. An important methodological work on these lines was

Terence W. Hutchison, *The Significance and Basic Postulates of Economic Theory* (London: Macmillan, 1938).

8. Knight, *On the History and Method of Economics*, 160.

9. T. W. Hutchison, *Significance and Basic Postulates*, 152-3.

10. M. Blaug, *The Methodology of Economics, or How Economists Explain* (Cambridge: Cambridge University Press, 1980), 93. See ibid. where Blaug approvingly cites a similar blast by Paul Samuelson.

11. See Fritz Machlup, "The Problem of Verification in Economics," *Southern Economic Journal* 22 (July 1955): 1-21.

12. Bruce Caldwell, *Beyond Positivism: Economic Methodology in the Twentieth Century* (London: George Allen and Unwin, 1982), 118-35.

13. *Hayek on Hayek*, 68.

14. F. A. Hayek, "Economics and Knowledge," *Economica* n.s., 4 (February 1937): 33-54; reprinted in *Hayek, Individualism and Economic Order* (London: Routledge and Kegan Paul, 1949), chapter 2.

15. *Hayek, Individualism and Economic Order*, 33. In oral remarks years later, Hayek emphasized that his paper had the intent of identifying the limited role of a priori reasoning in economics.

16. Professor Rizzo has drawn my attention to the section in HA, 23-27, entitled "The Alter Ego," which seems to reflect this perspective.

17. See Joseph A. Schumpeter, *History of Economic Analysis* (New York: Oxford University Press, 1954), 804f.

18. Gunnar Myrdal, *The Political Element in the Development of Economic Theory,* (Cambridge, Mass.: Harvard University Press, 1954). Machlup's review was in *American Economic Review* (December 1955).

19. Myrdal, 128.

20. See the republished text of Machlup's review in his *Methodology of Economics and Other Social Sciences,* 478.

Chapter Four

1. See Lionel C. Robbins, *The Nature and Significance of Economic Science,* 2nd edition (London: Macmillan, 1935), 101. See however J. A. Schumpeter, *History of Economic Analysis,* (Oxford and New York: Oxford University Press, 1954), 965, for a different attribution.

2. See Frank M. Machovec, *Perfect Competition and the Transformation of Economics,* (London and New York: Routledge, 1995).

3. Ludwig von Mises, "Profit and Loss," in *Planning for Freedom and Other Essays and Addresses,* 2nd edition (South Holland, Ill.: Libertarian Press, 1962), 109.

4. Ibid.

5. This section has not emphasized the role of entrepreneurial innovation in the Misesian market process. Certainly Mises

recognized the importance of innovation in the market process, and its entrepreneurial character. (See, for example, HA, 511-2; see also the passage cited above, at note 6). Unlike Schumpeter, however, Mises did not place innovation, as such, at the heart of his analysis of the market. For further discussion of the relationship between Misesian entrepreneurship and Schumpeterian (innovative) entrepreneurship, see this writer's *The Driving Force of the Market: Essays in Austrian Economics* (London and New York: Routledge, 2000), chapter 13.

6. See Israel M. Kirzner, *Competition and Entrepreneurship* (Chicago: University of Chicago Press, 1973).

7. "Catallactics" is the term Mises adopted (from the nineteenth-century economist Richard Whately) to describe the study of exchanges.

8. The Misesian process of entrepreneurial discovery is to be sharply distinguished from the modern neoclassical economics of search, pioneered by G. J. Stigler's 1962 paper, "The Economics of Information," *Journal of Political Economy* 69 (June 1962). In the economics of search, agents are assumed, at the very outset of analysis, to know exactly what it is they are looking for and what the costs and benefits of the search will be (at least in probabilistic terms). Search is then a deliberate, cost-benefit-controlled, production-of-information process. By contrast, Misesian entrepreneurial discov-

ery is serendipitous, expressing the flash of entrepreneurial insight and recognition that "senses" (without deliberate, cost-benefit-calculated search) where opportunities are to be found.

9. See particularly below, chapter 6.

10. On this see Israel M. Kirzner, "Mises and his Understanding of the Capitalist System," *Cato Journal* 19, no. 2 (fall 1999), reprinted as chapter 9 in Israel M. Kirzner, *The Driving Force of the Market.*

11. For further discussion of this writer's critique of alternative readings of the Misesian position, see chapter 12 in the writer's *Driving Force of the Market.*

12. This latter theme has been valuably emphasized by Joseph T. Salerno; see especially his "Mises and Hayek Dehomogenized," *Review of Austrian Economics* 6, no. 2, 113-46. For this writer's discussion, see further in *The Driving Force of the Market,* chapter 9.

Chapter Five

1. See the three longer essays translated by Bettina Bien-Greaves and published under the editorship of Percy L. Greaves as the volume *Ludwig von Mises, On the Manipulation of Money and Credit* (Dobbs Ferry, New York: Free Market Books, 1978). The more important of these essays was first published as a

monograph *Geldwertstabilisierung und Konjunkturpolitik* (Jena: Gustav Fisher, 1928).

2. On this see J. A. Schumpeter, *History of Economic Analysis* (New York: Oxford University Press, 1954), part 4, chapter 8 (and especially section 5).

3. This work was a new edition of the English translation (first published in 1934) of the second (1924) German-language edition of Mises' (1912) work, *Theorie des Geldes und der Umlaufsmittel.*

4. J. A. Schumpeter, *History of Economic Analysis,* 1083.

5. See Don Patinkin, *Money, Interest and Prices: An Integration of Monetary and Value Theory,* 2nd edition, (New York: Harper and Row, 1965), 573ff, n. D.

6. For relevant literature see: (a) Murray N. Rothbard, "The Austrian Theory of Money," in *The Foundations of Modern Austrian Economics,* ed. Edwin G. Dolan, (Kansas City: Sheed and Ward, 1976), 170f; (b) Karen I. Vaughn, "Critical Discussion of the Four Papers," in *The Economics of Ludwig von Mises: Toward a Critical Reappraisal,* ed. L. Moss (Kansas City: Sheed and Ward, 1976) 103; (c) Leland Yeager, *The Fluttering Veil, Essays on Monetary Disequilibrium* (Indianapolis: Liberty Fund, 1997), 152f.

7. Friedrich A. Hayek, *Prices and Production,* 2nd edition, (London: Routledge, 1935), 129.

8. F. A. Lutz, "On Neutral Money," in *Roads To Freedom: Es-*

says in Honor of Friedrich A. von Hayek, E. Streissler, G. Haberler, F. A. Lutz, and F. Machlup (London: Routledge and Kegan Paul, 1969), 105.

9. See Lutz, for the ambiguities surrounding the precise definition of the term.

10. On the success of this work, see Mises, TMC, 465; J. A. Schumpeter, *History of Economic Analysis,* 1091.

11. Schumpeter, *History of Economic Analysis,* 1091. For an admiring characterization of Knapp as an economic historian, see ibid., 811 n.

12. Ibid., 1091.

13. In the *Handwörterbuch der Staatswissenschaften.*

14. T. W. Hutchison, *A Review of Economic Doctrines, 1870-1929* (Oxford: Clarendon Press, 1953), 143.

15. For similar later assessments of Knapp's theory, see Schumpeter, 1090, and M. L. Burstein, *Modern Monetary Theory* (New York: St. Martin's Press, 1986), 3 (where Knapp is described as having "exercised great, mostly pernicious, influence").

16. Schumpeter, ibid.

17. This is part of an appendix added to the 1924, 2nd edition, of the book.

18. See Mises, *Money, Method and the Market Process,* 77, 86; Mises, preface to "Monetary Stabilization and Cyclical Policy [1929]" in *On the Manipulation of Money and Credit,* 59, 115.

See especially also the following statement in Ludwig von Mises, *The Historical Setting of the Austrian School of Economics* (New Rochelle, N.Y.: Arlington House, 1969), 41: "The interpretation of the causes...of the trade cycle which the present writer provided, first in his Theory of Money and Credit...was called by some authors the Austrian Theory of the Trade Cycle. Like all such national labels, this too is objectionable. The Circulation Credit Theory is a continuation, enlargement, and generalization of ideas first developed by the British Currency School and of some additions to them by later economists, among them also the Swede, Knut Wicksell."

19. F. A. Hayek, *Money, Capital, and Fluctuations; Early Essays,* edited by Roy McCloughry (Chicago: University of Chicago Press, 1984), 2.

20. See Hayek's preface to the 2nd edition of *Prices and Production,* xiii.

21. Ludwig M. Lachmann, "The Science of Human Action," *Economica* 18 (November 1951), 412-27; reprinted in Ludwig M. Lachmann, *Capital, Expectations, and the Market Process,* ed. W. E. Grinder (Kansas City: Sheed, Andrews and McMeel, 1977), 105.

22. "Money-substitutes" are "[c]laims to a definite amount of money, payable and redeemable on demand, against a debtor about whose solvency and willingness to pay there does not

prevail the slightest doubt." (Mises, HA, 432.)

23. For a recent discussion of differences between the Misesian and the Hayekian versions of the theory see Jean-Gabriel Bliek, "Hayek's Anti-Cycle Theory as the Rule of Necessity," in *Journal des Economistes et des Etudes Humaines,* 9, no. 4, (December, 1999) 589-607.

24. Gottfried Haberler, *Prosperity and Depression: A Theoretical Analysis of Cyclical Movements,* 3rd edition, (Lake Success, N.Y.: United Nations, 1946), 32f.

25. Mises, "Monetary Stabilization and Cyclical Policy" (1928), 141.

26. Mises, Ibid., 142.

27. Haberler, *Prosperity and Depression,* 65.

28. For a somewhat more detailed account of Mises' views on these topics, see Israel M. Kirzner, *Essays on Capital and Interest: An Austrian Perspective* (Cheltenham, UK and Brookfield: Elgar, 1996), essay 3.

29. *Economica* 8 (November 1941).

30. On this see the present writer's essay cited above, n. 27.

31. Keynes's influential work was *The General Theory of Employment, Interest and Money* (London: Macmillan, 1936).

32. See however the two essays, (originally published in 1948 and 1950, respectively), republished as chapter 4 ("Stones into Bread: The Keynesian Miracle") and chapter 5 ("Lord Keynes and Say's Law") in Ludwig von Mises, *Planning for*

Freedom and Other Essays and Addresses, 2nd edition, (South Holland, Ill.: Libertarian Press, 1962).

Chapter Six

1. For the relation between Mises' statement of the problems confronting economic calculation under socialism and Hayek's articulation of this problem in terms of dispersed knowledge (under socialism) of relevant scarcities, see Israel M. Kirzner, *The Driving Force of the Market,* chapter 8. There is no question that in the eyes of the public, Hayek was Mises' most articulate and influential supporter in regard to his critique of the economics of socialism.

2. For an account of the inter-war debate, see T. J. Hoff, *Economic Calculation in the Socialist Society* [translation of the 1938 Norwegian original] (London: William Hodge, 1949). For a superb account bringing the story up to the 1980s, see Don Lavoie, *Rivalry and Central Planning: The Socialist Calculation Debate Reconsidered* (Cambridge: Cambridge University Press, 1985).

3. On this see Don Lavoie, ibid.

4. In fact he had, already in 1929, published a work with the title *Kritik des Interventionismus* (Jena: Gustav Fischer, 1929).

5. For a full-length study of this kind of dynamic, see Sanford Ikeda, *Dynamics of the Mixed Economy, Toward a Theory of*

Interventionism (London and New York: Routledge, 1997).

6. Ludwig von Mises, "Middle-of-the-Road Policy Leads to Socialism," in *Planning for Freedom and other Essays and Addresses,* 22f.

7. The late Murray N. Rothbard was notable as the prominent follower and exponent of Mises who articulated a particularly strong form of unqualified libertarian philosophy. See especially his *For a New Liberty: The Libertarian Manifesto* (revised edition) (New York and London: Collier Macmillan, 1978). It should be noted that Rothbard did not subscribe to Mises' insistence on the need for (and possibility of) a sharp separation between the *wertfrei* propositions of economic science and the value-laden statements of political-philosophical discourse.

8. See also Mises, HA, 149: "The state is essentially an institution for the preservation of peaceful interhuman relations. However, for the preservation of peace it must be prepared to crush the onslaughts of peace-breakers."

9. We use here the term "classical liberalism" to distinguish it, of course, from what has, since before the middle of the twentieth century, been termed liberalism in the U.S. Mises generally used the term "liberalism" in what Leland Yeager refers to as "the European and etymologically correct sense of the word." See Yeager's *Introduction to Nation, State and Economy: Contributions to the Politics and History of Our Time*

[1919], by Ludwig von Mises (New York: New York University Press, 1983) xi.

10. William Baumgarth, "Ludwig von Mises and the Justification of the Liberal Order," in *The Economics of Ludwig von Mises: Toward a Critical Reappraisal,* ed. L. Moss (Kansas City: Sheed and Ward, 1976) 97.

11. See Mises, NR, 19f, for some hints of how, as a university student, Mises, who at first considered liberalism to be "an obsolete world view," came gradually to appreciate it.

12. This was the noble house, the Prussian electors and kings, from which sprang the German Kaisers.

13. In this, Mises' position was very similar to that of F. A. Hayek, whose 1944 *Road to Serfdom* pointed out the parallels between the "liberal" interventionist programs of the Western democracies and the roots of Nazi Germany. See also Hayek's essay, "Why I Am Not A Conservative," published as a postscript to F. A. Hayek, *The Constitution of Liberty* (Chicago: University of Chicago Press, 1960), 397-411.

14. Yeager, introduction to *Nation, State, and Economy,* xi.

15. George J. Stigler, "The Politics of Political Economists," *Quarterly Journal of Economics* (November 1959): 522-32.

16. The statement in the text certainly recognizes the role played, during the past four decades, by the (post-Knightian) Chicago School in nudging public opinion in the U.S. toward

a more favorable attitude toward free markets. In particular, Professor Milton Friedman (see especially his *Capitalism and Freedom* [Chicago: University of Chicago Press, 1962]) has exercised an influence far wider than that of Mises. Nonetheless, in terms of vigor, passion, and sheer consistency, the statement in the text should command general agreement. It should of course be noted that the economics underlying the Chicago School's pro-market positions is quite different from that of Mises. For Chicago, it is the assumption of rapid attainment by markets of results approximating those inherent in the model of perfectly competitive equilibrium that provides the analytical basis. As we have seen both in chapter 4 and in the present chapter, this was certainly *not* the basis for Mises' own positions.

Postscript

1. See above, chapter 6, n. 46.
2. Karen I. Vaughn, "The Rebirth of Austrian Economics: 1974-99," *Economic Affairs: Journal of the Institute of Economic Affairs,* 20, no. 1 (March 2000): 40-43.

INDEX